T0357641

"Most of us believe that we effectively particip: others, and in fact, we usually are trying to do there is much more to effective dialogue than w Danielle helps us enormously in teaching us the Nine Asks. In uncertain times, the community may be the answer, and effective dialogue is the vehicle to be in the community. *The Nine Asks* should be read by everyone interested in more sane and life-affirming communities."

—Phil Cass, CEO, Columbus Medical Association

"*The Nine Asks* clarified for me all that Danielle worked to achieve as she guided our organization to a better cultural state. I believe a higher level of cultural competency can be mastered in any organization if the resources and concepts described and developed in this book are intentionally applied. This is a must-have book for any leader wanting to improve their company's culture."

—Mike Johnson, superintendent, Liberty Union-Thurston Local Schools

"*The Nine Asks* is an invitation to a journey of personal and collective healing. I've seen firsthand how these principles can break down barriers and foster genuine connection, creating spaces where vulnerability thrives and understanding blossoms. This book is a must-read for anyone seeking to cultivate deeper relationships and build a more compassionate world."

—Amanda Golden, cofounder and managing principal, Designing Local

"Bold and transformative, *The Nine Asks* redefines how we grow, connect, and create safer spaces. Danielle offers a clear and practical framework that allows readers to embrace self-discovery, meaningful change, and true humanity. For lovers of wisdom and those devoted to practicing authentic connection, this book serves as a guiding light. When we trust the spaces we inhabit and the people within them as contributors to our journeys toward healing and wholeness, we unlock the power of our stories to effect real change and speak truth to power. Whether you're taking your first step or continuing a path of growth, this is where the journey deepens—for yourself and the world you impact."

—Tanya McClanahan, Senior Administrator for Education and Child Protection, Franklin County (Ohio) Children Services

"*The Nine Asks* is an important book that will allow you to discover you. Each agreement invites readers to embrace courage, humility, and accountability while navigating personal, cultural, social, and systemic dynamics. *The Nine Asks* equips you with actionable steps to be more—more authentic, more purposeful, more true. This book is your compass for transforming obstacles into opportunities and paving the way for a more inclusive and empowered future."
—Margaret Mitchell, CEO, YWCA USA

"*The Nine Asks* is a reckoning of innate deep dilemmas perpetuated by social stigmas and procedural practice. Danielle highlights the urgency of self-actualization while illuminating the realities of a dehumanizing society. Each chapter will cause you to pause in evaluating the state of our social emotional well-being while encouraging you to galvanize learning communities that protect these human experiences. This book is timely, necessary, and lifesaving!"
—Ruchelle L. Pride, director, Office of Justice Policy and Programs, CASA of Franklin County, Ohio

"We all want to be truly seen, heard, and loved in all aspects of our lives. *The Nine Asks* gives us a framework that, if practiced with humility, will build trust and courage in any relationship. This is not just a book that you read, put down, and then you're done. It's a manuscript to incorporate into our daily life practices for changing how we show up for others."
—Chip Spinning, executive director, Franklin County (Ohio) Children Services

"Danielle's book is a must-read road map to being your authentic self. An inspiring book with lessons for a lifetime."
—Stephanie Hightower, president and CEO, Columbus Urban League

THE NINE ASKS

KIMBERLY DANIELLE

THE NINE ASKS

Creating Safer and More Courageous Spaces

WESTMINSTER
JOHN KNOX PRESS
LOUISVILLE · KENTUCKY

© 2025 Kimberly Danielle

First edition
Published by Westminster John Knox Press
Louisville, Kentucky

25 26 27 28 29 30 31 32 33 34—10 9 8 7 6 5 4 3 2 1

All rights reserved. No part of this book may be reproduced or transmitted in any form or by any means, electronic or mechanical, including photocopying, recording, or by any information storage or retrieval system, without permission in writing from the publisher. For information, address Westminster John Knox Press, 100 Witherspoon Street, Louisville, Kentucky 40202-1396. Or contact us online at www.wjkbooks.com.

Scripture quotations are from *The Holy Bible, English Standard Version*, copyright © 2001 by Crossway Bibles, a publishing ministry of Good News Publishers. Used by permission. All rights reserved.

Book design by Drew Stevens
Cover design by Marc Whitaker / MTWdesign.net

Library of Congress Cataloging-in-Publication Data is on file at the
Library of Congress, Washington, DC.

ISBN: 978-0-664-26755-1 (paperback)
ISBN: 978-1-646-98422-0 (ebook)

Most Westminster John Knox Press books are available at special quantity discounts when purchased in bulk by corporations, organizations, and special-interest groups. For more information, please e-mail SpecialSales@wjkbooks.com.

To Estie, for exemplifying safety, unwavering protection, support to the point of sacrifice, and most of all, for giving and being everything I never knew I needed to feel at home

To my lineage, whose provision of ancestral wisdom, supernatural covering, and intragenerational prayers endlessly affirm my purpose and continual healing

Trigger Warning
There is sensitive content in this book that may trigger the reader, including references to racism, sexism, grief, community violence, police violence, childhood neglect, child trauma, family trauma, bullying, physical abuse, and suicidal ideation. If you encounter a topic that is emotionally challenging, it may manifest in feelings of discomfort and upset. Please take this warning into consideration. Your holistic wellness matters.

CONTENTS

Part Three: Application of the Nine Asks

PART ONE
CREATING
THE CONTAINER

CHAPTER 1

Why Sharing Stories Matters

The Nine Asks were born from "the village"—the strangers, neighbors, friends, and family we do life with every day. In 2010, I hosted my first learning community as an administrator in a college setting with about twenty-five very demographically different people on the theme of identity and belongingness. Before we commenced conversation and the yearlong experience, I asked what participants needed to feel authentic and to be themselves. They looked puzzled and stunned by the inquiry. Some were immediately uncomfortable. In retrospect, I presume they desired and expected to have good conversations but had no expectation of—or practice with—how to be real and go deeper in fellowship with strangers. However, the only way for genuine community spaces to be archievable is for the container to transform into more than a surface-level conversation in a random moment. We had to be different, and we had to do something different. We had to be better versions of ourselves *for* ourselves and one another.

The good news is that these kinds of experiences are not exclusive to academia. There is an invitation for these moments to happen all around us, all the time. If it is true that we can constantly learn and evolve in the practice of being human, it could be proposed that all shared spaces with other people are like "learning communities."

In these learning communities, we pull apart and put back together different layers of our identities. We do so through the application of tools to enrich conversation and reflection. We slow down our thinking and learning mode to look a little deeper into our personal stories, especially as they relate to our multifaceted and intersectional lenses through which we make meaning of and understand the world. The better we understand ourselves and one another, the better odds we have of being more "radically compassionate" (in the words of Dr. Tara Brach) and more just with ourselves and one another.

One of the many challenges in the practice of social justice work; diversity, equity, and inclusion (DEI) work; or healing work is being asked or expected to make the learning opportunities as quick, succinct, and surface-level as possible. Some want the work of building the container and making spaces safer, braver, and more courageous to be something that can be checked off a to-do list. How does one talk about trauma in an hour? What is the best approach to facilitate a conversation on implicit bias and systemic oppression in a way that will not offend the delicate nature of someone considered to have disproportionately larger amounts of privilege and status? When is a good time to point out when someone or something is moving in a way that is cognitively dissonant? How does one get from point A to point B in spiritual evolution without getting dirty and messy along the healing journey?

The Nine Asks are not simply a list of words on a piece of paper to be posted on a wall and referenced in case of a human-systems emergency. The Nine Asks is a living, breathing document. It is not a set of instructions for what to do when we get ourselves in trouble with other sentient beings but rather a way of being.

Why Trauma-Informed Social Justice?

Deep virtues and principles have become meaningless clichés to which we have lost relationship and connection. The African principle "it takes a village to raise a child" became a presidential campaign slogan. Technologies and businesses have been named after ancestral cultures and philosophies. Similarly, the lexicon for how to engage with other humans has become too overpopulated with jargon. Once a taboo and intriguing idea, "cultural competence" now has certificate programs and graduate-level coursework in business management curriculum for those interested in the business case for learning how to honor people and heritage. We attempt to "teach" people to be sensitive, tolerant, and accepting. Businesses can't even agree on proper and universally acceptable terminology, differentiating from cultural competence to cultural sensitivity to cultural humility. Whole departments now exist under the name of DEI or some blend of those words, implying warmth and concern for justice, but their execution typically resembles the most widely accepted and palatable version of human engagement work in the form of policies, practices, and procedures. While cultural competence and DEI efforts are a sign of progress, I implore folks to understand that this is only half of the job of honoring sentient beings. Cultural competence and DEI initiatives may address the present and future experiences people have in human spaces, but it does not address the much-needed attention of the wounds people already possess mentally, physically, and emotionally.

One strategy is not enough in navigating human spaces with effective compassion. Integrative approaches come closer to recognizing the complexity of our experiences and ways of belonging to one another. The act of using resources, services, and frameworks to address the hurts and harms of a person's past is a trauma-informed approach. Additionally, DEI may efficiently create a platform for recognizing folks' identities and unique needs. However, DEI often fails to take into consideration the presence and role of privilege and power and the ways in which both social structures can be misused and abused. Social justice takes matters of DEI a step further by creating space for the acknowledgment of both one's identity and needs as well as one's invisibility and denial of needs caused by disenfranchisement and disempowerment. Through infusion of both principles, trauma-informed approaches *plus* social justice efforts apply approaches, frameworks, services, and resources for individual, collective, and universal healing and resilience. When we trust a space and the people within it as contributors to and supporters of our journeys to be healthy, healed, and whole, we can better utilize our stories for good and change the world by speaking truth to power.

The Gift of Giving Our Stories

The first opportunity we are given to begin our own story-sharing process is in personal introductions. Arguably our most powerful moments exist in saying our names and declaring with pride and absolution who we are. Altruistically, we have the agency to tell people who we are and how we show up in the world the moment we open our mouths to speak. However, what we typically do, particularly in the career-driven and object-oriented culture of the United States, is tell people what we do or what we have. Whether coming across a new colleague at a conference, a fellow employee in the workspace, or even a passerby in leisure spaces, we often begin our exchange with others by asking, "What do you do?," or we volunteer information about our job. This is especially true if we believe that our job is important or fulfilling. However, our jobs are not *who* we are; they are *what* we do. Our jobs give us access to money so that we can pay bills. Sharing this information does not give someone a broader sense of what we believe we have been called to do in the world and why we say yes to that calling on a regular basis. We intentionally engage in superficial conversation because it's easier.

Chances are you have had a mentor or an elder instruct you to keep your personal and professional lives separate. This training has aided humans in being well prepared to share our success stories. We share all the lotus and none of the mud. All the roses and none of the thorns. All the beauty and none of the ashes. One could argue that the creation of social media platforms has exacerbated superficial, surface-level, and transactional communication. We may not know someone's motivation for life, their deepest inspiration, or the twinkle in their eyes that makes them genuinely smile. However, through social media and networking platforms, they may share where they work, what their title is, what they studied in school, and their level of educational attainment. Depending on one's comfort and transparency, we may even have an idea of the kind of home someone has, how their family members look, what kinds of objects and entertainment they spend their money on, and maybe a rough idea of their income bracket. While this information may give us context clues about an individual's book cover, it does not give us insight into the soul of their story.

The ugly truth is that most of us, by the time we reach adulthood, no longer seek a deep connection with folks. We reach a certain age and decide we have enough friends. Transactional conversation with acquaintances becomes exhausting. We don't even respond authentically to the standard inquiry, "How are you?" It takes too long to share. Nobody wants to hear the truth anyway. And depending on the level of drama and trauma in our families and histories, we even, at times, hide from toxic blood relatives and complicated friendships to delay or deny the risk of disappointment. Who wants to go through the discomfort of sharing your story, only to be obligated to other people's "stuff" in response and return? Sometimes it is difficult to face your own issues, let alone trusting and believing someone else will be properly equipped to hold space for your story. Adulting and human existence in general can be overwhelming. As one of my friends and colleagues often says, "People do what they can." We are capable of managing only so much physically, socially, emotionally, and spiritually. Once we reach the limit of what we can handle, the residue slips from our hands. Understanding emotional capacity on a basic level, we can find it challenging to entrust the innermost secrets and stories of who we are with folks whom we perceive to be neither interested nor able to handle the truth of what lies behind our masks.

The sticky wicket of not wanting other people's stories and not wanting to share our own stories is that it sentences us to the imprisonment of doing life with one another in ambiguity and cluelessness. I never truly get to know you, and you never truly get to know me. Therefore, it makes it almost impossible for you to treat me with care, love, and respect; and vice versa. It's easier for you to hurt me if you don't know me. If you perceive me as a stranger who is wholly and completely disconnected from you, you have no incentive for extending empathy and compassion. Instead, your representative crosses paths with my representative, neither of whom is our most authentic selves. We transactionally interact with each other and hope to get our basic needs met without seeking a relationship. We just want to be left alone in an existence where our neighbors don't know us. We avoid social interaction. We text instead of talk. We avoid all opportunities to have genuine connection with others. We miss the mark of the experiment being social creatures. Ultimately, you don't know me, you don't trust me, and you are incapable of knowing my value or worth as it relates to who I am, why I exist, and what I believe my purpose is. You may know what you see on the outside, but without meaning or context from me, you will never know my why.

Why is it so difficult for us to share our struggle and survival stories? Are we afraid of being disappointed by others? Do we fear embarrassment if folks discover we're mortal and imperfect? Are we afraid of looking and sounding weak? Are we blocking the risk of feeling heaviness, shame, and guilt from which we have not yet healed?

What if, in telling our stories of loneliness, it made us feel *less* alone? What if sharing our struggle and survival stories frees us *and* someone else in the process? Could our stories be the levies that need to break and release the raging waters of the storms inside of us? Might we be good Samaritans through our stories with lighthouse anecdotes that serve as warnings for folks who are lost in darkness and need guidance to navigate a way to safety? Could the telling of our tales make us better bystanders? Is it possible that our survival imparted us with a responsibility to tell others that experiences are indeed survivable? What if the power to heal yourself and others exists partly by speaking the truth about your battles—won and lost—and how you made it over?

Receiving Stories with Grace and Gratitude

I can hear it now. Someone reading this has likely comforted a friend or loved one in said person's time of need and kindly extended the invitation to "call me whenever you need to talk!" You may have even been sincere . . . in that moment. Then the hour of need passed. A new day dawned, and on this new day, you have depleted your desire to be a support system. After your special moment of assistance and advocacy had its sunrise and sunset, have you ever evaded human contact as if you were the sole survivor in an elementary school dodgeball game? Have you ever avoided a phone call or ignored a text or email message because you didn't want to obligate yourself to listening to someone talk? Are you reading this chapter right now instead of getting back to someone who believes you were really going to "call right back"? I get it; you're not alone.

It takes a ready mind and spirit to hold space for someone, especially if the conversation could be long or difficult. As adults, we manage so much to try to be well. At the end of a long day or a full week, we may have very little capacity to "get it right" in each of our relationships. But when and where we are able to listen, we can practice being *better* listeners. If someone has entrusted us with their story, we have essentially been asked to do more than just listen; we have been chosen as a recipient of the gift of their story. The sharing of deeper thoughts, feelings, and emotions is a sacred practice, and the gift of receiving these virtues should be honored as such.

As laborious as it may feel to hold space for someone, there will be moments when we must be present and do the work of centering someone else's voice. Sometimes it's not about us. We forget how incredibly difficult it is for someone to share. We might miss that when we have been chosen as a listener of someone's story, they are simultaneously choosing to be brave and courageous through vulnerability. It took guts for them to say *anything* at all. Are we up to the task of being worthy of their trust? Further, how do we equip ourselves to hold space compassionately and empathetically for a story of struggle and survival in a trauma-informed way?

Here are three suggestions on how to be gracious receivers when we receive the gift of hearing—and learning from—others' trauma stories:

1. *Receive the story as their truth.* Perception is reality. When hearing someone's story, the struggle or suffering they share may not sound as devastating to us. The solution or path to survival might be simpler, in our opinions, than what the storyteller might see. It's not our job to fact-check or verify elements of the story. We have no right to assume they are exaggerating, blowing the experience out of proportion, or being dramatic. Being a trauma-informed person means

no gaslighting. (Gaslighting is a form of psychological manipulation where an individual tries to confuse or convince their target that what they felt or experienced is not real.) We have no right to tell someone their trauma did or did not happen. It means not giving opinions on whether we believe a person was right or wrong. We were not asked to critique folks' lived experiences; we were asked to listen, and we were trusted to hold space. Listen. Hold space. That's it.

2. *Do not give suggestions or advice (unless asked).* No one knows a person's story better than the person who lived it. How can we begin to tell a person what they should have done? How they could have better responded? What they should have noticed or perceived? And the absolute no-no: what we would have done. In the moment someone shares their story with us, be present in noticing there is a sentient being with feelings sitting in front of us, asking us to show up for them with empathy and compassion. It's not our story; it's their story, and they are sharing what happened. Past tense. Our job is to support them in the present tense.

3. *Keep the storyteller centered in their story.* It is possible that there could be instances when a story is shared with us, and it triggers our own thoughts, feelings, memories, and emotions. Their hurt might remind us of hurt we have felt and might even take us back to the pain. It is also within the realm of possibility that their pain might recall ways that we caused someone harm. It is human nature to not want to imagine ourselves as the perpetrator of pain or the recipient of pain. Though it can be difficult, we must regulate ourselves enough to have empathy without making the moment about us. We must find a way to show compassion and understanding even in moments when we want to defend ourselves or others in the story. We must remember this is not our story. We are the receivers, and the storyteller is the author as well as the main character.

It has become easier to believe there is no worth or value in deeper connection, but that's not true. In the spirit of the Zulu principle of Ubuntu, which believes "I am a person through the existence of other people," we must believe in the power of being connected to and impacted by one another. Humanity is worth the labor of creating safer spaces. And those spaces are reliant on our investment in our stories — and one another.

CHAPTER 2

Why Feeling Safe Matters

Societal norms have informed and perhaps at times indoctrinated us to believe we are safe in the care of friends, leaders, and elders who are part of our families, communities, and sacred spaces. Of the many virtues whose composite totals define our individual and collective morals and ethics, safety might arguably be one of the most important. The feeling of safety grounds us. In other words, it gives us a sense of balance and strong foundation. Is there any wonder why the foundational levels of Maslow's hierarchy of needs pyramid includes physiological needs like air, water, food, and clothing, and then safety? Self-actualization is not possible if I do not feel safe. Personal value and success are not achievable if I am not safe enough to believe I can excel. I cannot love myself or others, at least not well, if safety is not present in relationships. Although safety is core to our needs as human beings, safety is a more nebulous thing than we might realize. It cannot be universally defined; it is person specific. In this chapter, I will ask you to reflect on your personal narrative of safety and security, including your earliest memories of feeling safe and protected. You will be presented with opportunities to pause through guided imagery and reflection questions on what makes you feel safe and to identify possible ancestral memories for your personal definitions of safety.

One of my hopes during our time together as you read this book is to gain your confidence and help you open up to some of the concepts beneath the Nine Asks. That said, you do not know me. Asking you for that kind of vulnerability might require me to give a little of myself to earn your trust, and I am willing to do that. (By the way, this is a sneak peek of me modeling Ask #1 with you!) In addition to providing guided imagery and reflection questions, I will share personal and professional lived experiences where application of the Nine Asks helped promote trust and safety—or could have, had they been properly utilized. Later in this chapter, I will begin sharing personal reflections on some community activism efforts in response to the killing of two Black men in my hometown by law enforcement personnel. My advocacy and activism work are most often actualized in service as a healer and support person to other organizers, activists, community, and family members who are survivors of injustice. Therefore, everything I do must be grounded in creating and retaining safer, braver, and more courageous personal and shared spaces. Cultural competence alone is only a partial approach to inclusionary and trust-building practices. I continually learn through my relationships with others that I must try to the best of my abilities to live a life that embodies the everyday practice of the Nine Asks. The Nine Asks are about building genuine trust; and trust creates pathways for mutual safety.

Do No Harm

When we walk into a classroom or a doctor's office, we may feel comfort in knowing our teachers and physicians took an oath to "do no harm." Although there are always exceptions, we typically do not enter educational and medical spaces with the expectation of being hurt or harmed. It is my hope that parents, guardians, faith-based leaders, politicians, and other individuals deemed as community leaders with some measure of power, control, and privilege in (and at times over) the lives of others have also made a commitment to do no harm to those they serve. In essence, a promise to do no harm is a commitment to do one's best in keeping others safe. If you are in a position of power over me and if I trust you will do no harm to me, I am entrusting you to be a watchman of my safety, security, and protection. I believe that while I am in your care, no danger will come to me. This belief purports that safety takes into consideration a practice of equality. I would instead strongly suggest that safety requires the applied practice of equity. Equality gives everyone the same thing, while equity gives everyone specifically what they need. You might know what *you* need to feel safe because you already know who you are. If you do not know who I am authentically or what my past and present story is, how could you possibly know what I require to feel safe and out of harm's way?

How early does the personal narrative of safety begin to take form? Experts in trauma and resilience such as Dr. Bessel van der Kolk and Dr. Peter A. Levine might suggest that our first inklings of safety begin before we are even born. What if we are biologically designed and hardwired with natural instincts as to what our preferred sensations for safety and well-being are? What if our bodies and minds are engrafted with a baseline understanding of what it feels like to be nurtured, safe, and protected?

Safety stories, prayerfully, start with small, implicit exemplars of protection and well-being—even in utero. Picture an unborn child weeks before delivery, napping in the belly of its mother. Its senses are already at work. What is the baby experiencing? The tight fold of limbs neatly tucked away into themselves and nestled into its core. The muffled soft vocal timbre of its mother's voice on the other side of smooth skin, stretched like the top of a worn-in djembe drum. The metronome of a whooshing heartbeat, predictably in accompaniment with the hammock-like swing of a warm womb, lulling baby with every step its mom makes. Its instinct is to suckle for both comfort and nourishment. And amid the soothing sensory stimulants, the baby sleeps soundly. Most sentient beings might feel calmer and safer in imagining, through this visualization, the experience of an in utero baby. Before we are born, our narratives of safety begin to take form.

Some of us, during childhood and young adulthood, might have acquired nicknames from friends and family members who loved and cared for us. We were christened with monikers to remember people, moments, or memories, and we belong to each other through the understanding that "only you can call me this name because its meaning belongs to both of us." As we grow up and older, we learn melodies and music that become the soundtracks to important and meaningful moments in our lives and histories. We archive in our chests and spirits the songs that make us brave when we need to feel fearless, seen and understood when we feel broken, and wail of hurt and rage when we ourselves cannot express on our own in words. From the moment we develop a relationship with a song, within a few bars, we can be whisked away to a single moment in time where we were genuine, authentic, and real in our skin. There is a spirit in language and music, one that hurts as well as heals.

In our early years, we begin moving about the planet, believing all who we encounter share our definitions, meanings, and understandings of life's virtues, which include security and safety. Surely, we all agree about what respect looks like, what happiness is, and what makes us feel safe, right? If we are fortunate enough to be reared within secure and functional households, we are likely to start life in relationship with at least one person who we believe loves us and seeks to protect us from harm. Rude awakenings begin as early as the elementary school playground when we encounter folks who do not know—and do not care to know—who we truly are and what we need to feel secure. In fact, when insecurity is present in individuals (both child and adult), it is likely that said insecure individuals will become less focused on others' safety and well-being and more intent on preserving and protecting their own safety and well-being.

A loving family or household may have encouraged its members to foster relationships with strangers (e.g., "I made a new friend today!"). We are, after all, designed to be social. As we grow up and grow older, we gravitate further away from the goal of relationship-building and more toward transactional interactions in the interest of gaining an object we desire or completing a task we are charged to perform. In either case, the human being with whom we are called to interact is removed from empathetic consideration in the equation. This is a far journey away from our original understanding of safety for self and others. Outside a lens of collective safety, if I do not know you, if I do not understand you, or—worst-case scenario—if I believe you are a threat to my ability to survive the moment unharmed, the likelihood increases that I might be a threat of harm to you.

Through space, movement, words, tones, volumes, relationships, and many other factors, we customize our safety stories. We create the rubric, as specific as our DNA and our fingerprints, for what makes us feel seen, heard, felt, understood, and appreciated. This is how we personally come to understand safety. What is even more incredible is that the notion of safety does not just live in our minds; it also lives in our bodies. The meaning can become a cognitive, social, spiritual, and a somatic (or body) experience. We do not just experience safety as a thought; we implicitly or unconsciously understand what it means to be safe throughout our whole bodies and through the intake of all our senses.

Stakes Are High

What happens when we combine our individual, constructed stories of safety with power, control, and privilege in shared human systems like working spaces, learning spaces, worship spaces, and other collective environments? What are the ramifications, if any, of my personal lens on what it means to be safe and sound? Let's isolate the sense of sound as an example of how personal and specific our understanding of safety can be.

Imagine two households with young children: Child A and Child B. Child A's household is filled with siblings, a flow of extended family members, televisions, and screens of smart devices projecting electric blue lights in the air. Laughter, arguments, and general presence of voices are heard from early morning until well into the evening. Buzzing of toys reverberate in hallways, and a seemingly constant clanking of dishes rings from the kitchen. Meanwhile, Child B has a completely different experience. Let us envision the latter youth is an only child. Their parents have quieter hobbies, such as reading books, doing crossword puzzles, or making crafts. There are very few people or "foot traffic" in the household of three (mom, dad, and child), and generally speaking, the only sounds Child B becomes accustomed to are the hums of the HVAC system whispering from the floor vents, clothes tumbling in the dryer, and the occasional pulsing beep of an efficiently warmed-up microwave meal.

Now imagine two teachers with similar sonic childhood backgrounds as Child A and Child B in a school building. Using solely the sense of sound, how might each teacher construct their classrooms? In considering personal social constructs through sound, think about how each teacher might perceive the behavior patterns of a well-behaved student. How might each teacher's relationship with sound impact their method of regulating or calming down anxious students? We might assume that a teacher with a background like Child B appreciates silence. They might design the classroom with nooks, zones, and intentionally created areas for students to have personal time to be alone. Discipline issues worth correction according to this teacher might include talking out of turn, tapping, banging on desks with pencils or fists, and humming or singing during silent reading. An ideal classroom in the mind of this teacher might include but not be limited to lamps versus fluorescent lights, plants near windows, silence during test taking, individual mats or rugs for children to sit on, and desks arranged in small pods.

Meanwhile, envision a teacher with a background much like that of Child A. Again, in applying only the sense of sound, how might this teacher's classroom differ from that of the aforementioned example? A teacher whose childhood was full of audible stimulants might have a high tolerance for a variety of sounds. They might design a classroom with furniture where students could sit and gather in groups, even during individual activities. Worthwhile discipline issues by this teacher's standards might begin with physical fighting, use of curse words, or destruction of property. An aesthetically ideal classroom in the mind of the teacher who shared an upbringing like Child A might include but not be limited to bright photos or posters on the walls, fluorescent and other bright lights, music during test taking, one large circle for student dialogue, and shared tables instead of desks.

Both teachers in these scenarios designed their classroom culture and climate based on what they believed to be the best approach to gifting their students with an ideal learning environment. Both individuals likely desired their students to feel comfortable, safe, protected, and inspired. However, are both classrooms conducive to the ideal comfort and safety of *every* student? Would a child who views their busy household as fun and exciting feel comfortable in a classroom where they were expected to sit still and silent unless called on to speak? Would a child who enjoys the stillness and silence of a quiet household be able to concentrate during a test if music is playing? What dictates safety for one student could very easily create an environment threatening to ideal learning for another student because each child (and teacher) has defined safety from their personal lens of experiences. This scenario calls us to question environments we may be creating for others—environments that are, in fact and truth, built to cater to *our* individual definitions of safety as opposed to a negotiated collective space and understanding of what everyone in the shared setting might need to feel safe, comfortable, and affirmed. If my ideal space is designed in opposition to or in conflict of what you need, I have inadvertently invited you into a setting that might easily be perceived as threatening, toxic, or hostile. Any setting that disrupts a person's ability to feel safe and secure could result in the experience of trauma.

For many people, use and application of the "T" word in situations and circumstances where there is no death, destruction, or mayhem present feels like an exaggerated use of the term. Few people desire to believe they were traumatized or, worse, are still manifesting traumatic signs, symptoms, and behaviors from past experiences or memories. We all want to believe we are or can be holistically well. We want to consider ourselves survivors and conquerors of challenges in life but without blemish, bruise, or scar from the hard knocks. Those who have either experienced extraordinarily few debilitating experiences or are physiologically disconnected from their deep hardships become irritated when trauma is used to describe an element of their story. Perhaps the notion of having trauma is perceived to be a weakness or evidence of a lack of grit. Meanwhile, others who know all too well that trauma is the most appropriate term for their stories also grimace when the topic emerges. Hapless souls with old shrapnel in their bodies are familiar with the impending jolt of pain on the way when they are reminded that they survived something—but barely.

Speaking of trauma in public places sometimes feels like uttering a curse word in the presence of people who believe themselves to be holy. It sometimes feels like a declaration of semantic war. I envision the pin of the grenade still clenched in my teeth as my mouth tightly pulls to one side. The word *trauma* is a live explosive I push off my lips and toss like a pitcher on the mound. Its bounce echoes in a crash on ceramic tile floor. While innocent victims in the vicinity attempt to dive for cover and protection behind behemoth inanimate objects, seconds tick in slow motion; then the room is engulfed by a sonic boom. Nature sways at the word's power, trees and shrubs plucked from earth, as mighty oaks become mulch in its wake. Trauma's heat and winds disintegrate brick and skin and sky like dust particles dancing in sunbeams. And after trauma dissipates, breaks away, and expends its power on our bodies, it is thought to disappear in the stratosphere, leaving everything in its pathway forever changed. . . . Or at least that is what we have been taught to believe.

Trauma, by definition, is a deeply distressing experience. Though it is, at times, a significantly horrific event, such as a natural disaster, a travesty of man's inhumanity to man, or constructs like systemic oppression, more times than not, trauma is personal; it is internal. It is our own private little hell. Trauma is a person-specific experience, meaning even in a shared memory or experience, one individual out of many may survive a moment with deep distress; meanwhile, others who experienced the same scenarios in the same moment may have no lasting distress at all. Many more of us battle small and menacing (but deeply distressful and dysregulating) experiences. Instead of a swift but significant stab with a samurai sword, imagine death by a thousand papercuts.

Life or Death Safety

What about the times, though, when mental trauma and the absence of safer spaces morph into life-threatening circumstances? I am writing a book on the principle of asking others to honor what we need to feel safer, braver, and courageous enough to let us be our whole and full selves at a time when it is, again, dangerous, to be othered in the United States. The irony is not lost on me that I began writing *The Nine Asks* in the winter of 2020 while living in my hometown of Columbus, Ohio, during the same month two Black men were killed by law enforcement within three weeks of each other. It, too, was hard not to notice that both Black men who were killed looked like family members of mine. This time, by the grace of God, it was not a biological family member of mine; but it *could* have been. These Black men were not safe, and they lost their lives via deadly force while interacting with public servants who took oaths to serve and protect the community. Even in death, the Black men still were not safe as their reputations and characters were cross-examined by the public and the courts during the investigations of their murders. They were not safe while they were living; they were not safe after their deaths. Are any of us safe, especially those of us who have been othered, who are misunderstood, or who are living in racialized Black bodies? I feel powerless and cosmically disrupted along with my community, family, and friends as we add the names of Casey Goodson Jr. and Andre Hill to the long list of people whose lives were cut short, implicitly in part, because their skin was too dark, their lips were too full, their noses were too broad, or their hair curl pattern was too tight.

Mindfully and meaningfully creating safer, braver spaces is the simplest but most complicated form of justice work. Referring to justice work as "tough" is a tremendous understatement. Healing, equity, and justice efforts take a toll on you if you are not holistically well. If you want to survive justice work, be resilient and normal on the other side (whatever "normal" is); you must know how to create and re-create safety sustainably, both inside and outside of your body. I know what it looks and feels like to not feel safe in your body. Before living out the Nine Asks in a trauma-informed way, I nearly drowned in the tide of not feeling safe enough to show up as my whole self. I have lost loved ones who did not feel safe enough in their bodies, minds, and spirits to battle the heaviness of laboring for human beings and against systemic oppression. MarShawn McCarrel and Amber Evans—creatives and comrades in Columbus, Ohio, whom we lost to suicide within three years of each other—were some of the most beautiful justice warriors I have ever known. The feeling still hurts and haunts me that they may not have known or felt the safety their spirits needed to fight another day.

How can I begin to write about how we can have more culturally responsive and more trauma-informed relationships with one another as sentient beings when my job security is directly connected to responding to man's inhumanity to man? I have dedicated my life to working toward making spaces feel safer and braver. Meanwhile, if an emergency were to take place and I needed immediate safety and protection, the very last call I would feel confident in making would be to law enforcement. I do not want that statement to be true. I want to believe that in a life-or-death situation, the gravest of all threats, I would be in good care with law enforcement. However, in a time such as this, I find myself in dialogue with my young, bright, and impressionable daughters about what to do to keep their bodies and minds intact should they ever come in contact with the police. My daughters, as young Black women, fear being stopped by the police more than they fear situations and scenarios where police should be called to serve and protect them. What would it take for my daughters to trust again? How can I convince you to care enough about others that you would sacrifice some element of your own safety to ensure someone else feels safer in your presence? What must we ask of the world and one another—and believe we will receive—to feel safer, braver, and more courageous to be who we are, wherever we are?

My mother, at the time of this writing, is a seventy-something-year-old Black woman who integrated the Catholic church and Catholic schools in Columbus, Ohio. She endured a great amount of racism during the decades-long experience. She later married into a white family, only for a couple years, but silently battled with a racist father-in-law. Though my mother is an Air Force veteran who served stateside during the Vietnam War, she has post-traumatic stress disorder (PTSD) not from military service but from integrating schools. The wound of that first integration never really went away. This community elder lived through the civil rights movement, easily recalling lived experiences from the Martin Luther King Jr. and John F. Kennedy assassination announcements and news coverage of the massacre march on the Edmund Pettus Bridge and the landmark Loving case that made interracial marriages—including her own—legal. Threat and danger—whether perceived or imminent—were the common denominators of my mother's existence. I was raised by a woman who has never felt fully safe a day in her life.

Recently while conducting a virtual workshop on cultural competence and trauma-informed approaches to working and learning, my mother overheard a discussion I was leading. As is often the case when the "room" gets brave enough for honest and vulnerable conversation to break out, the topic of racial implicit bias reared its ugly head. I facilitated and navigated the conversation as directly but delicately as possible and, in the end, my hope was that folks were able to finish the meeting and return to their regularly scheduled lives a little more open and ideally a little less fearful than before. That day, though, there was an unexpected, wounded bystander: my mother. After my session was over, she shuffled her slipper-covered feet into the den, plopped down in a chair, and stared off, baffled, searching for the right words. Her tired eyes peered at me over drugstore reading glasses. I inquired as to the reason for her confusion. In a hurt and puzzled voice seeking understanding, my mother pushed away long, mixed-gray dreadlocks and asked, "I thought we did this already?" The "this" to which she was referring was the war for equity. She spoke of discrimination she had endured throughout the years, fearing her battered and bruised spirit was a useless casualty of a war for compassion. "We already did this." Her words simmered in my chest like a stew on the back burner of a stove. How do you explain to an alumna of integration who still has Jim Crow keloids that some of us are still trying to show people with power and privilege how to be compassionate and empathetic to othered others? Yes, we stand on the shoulders of elders who paved the way and used their bodies and souls as foundation for "civil" rights and arguably equal quality of life safety measures we supposedly have in place. Those same elders are devastated to now witness a second coming of the same hatred, bigotry, violence, and threat to justice they thought they defeated many years ago. The world, again—or perhaps still—is not a safe place for everyone.

I cannot fathom the dangers that existed during the prime years of my mother's life. Her father was murdered when she was only five years old. She lived through arguably some of the most violent decades in recent history, including the social justice movement of the 1960s, two wars, and national economic collapses. I am certain my mother never imagined that her grandchildren would be born into a world of school shootings and then somehow adjust to a new normal when the invention of social media makes it possible for them to see and share the killings of innumerable Black people at the hands of community leaders they were originally taught were the good guys. Black and Brown children in particular are transitioning into adulthood and using social contexts and constructs to make meaning of the fact that they might not survive an interaction with law enforcement. When dialing 9-1-1 becomes a threat to one's safety, how on earth can we make a conversation feel safe? If I cannot ensure that my fellow brother or sister should feel secure enough to believe they can survive a traffic stop, how do I go about convincing them it is safe to build camaraderie with strangers? If we thought it was difficult to build general trust prior to the last twenty years, everything just got that much harder. It might arguably be true that many in the world and especially in the United States have not felt their safety and security threatened to this degree in a long time.

What baffles me is understanding that this dire state of paranoia in merely existing is not a true lived experience for everyone. We are all, in fact, living vastly different lives. It is a reminder that the definition, components, and measurements of safety are indeed specific to personal lived experiences. The fact that we are still debating the inequity of safety, especially in racialized bodies, is an almost unbearable burden to carry and attempt to defend. The burden of inequity in safety, however, is real, and I feel it in my own immediate family; sometimes I feel it in my own body.

If I were to receive a call about my Black brother being stopped by the police, I would instantly panic, manifesting my dysregulation physiologically through nausea, tense muscles, a headache, and sweaty palms. My first question would be, "Is he OK?" (Think about that for a second. If my brother were stopped by the police, my instinctive assumption would be of him being harmed as opposed to being helped.) I would be petrified of my brother's quick temper as a harbinger of hazard to his body. If he did make it out of a police force stop safely, my deeper and lingering concerns would be about how much pride, dignity, integrity, and authenticity he had to swallow to get home with no incident. Meanwhile, if I received the same call about my white father being stopped by the police, my assumption would be that my father was already home safe. In all honesty, I cannot be certain I would have any somatic reaction at all. My dad's white skin is both his and my assumed insurance policy that in most scenarios, he is safe. My father does not have to ask to be protected; it is presumed he already is.

Not until I began writing this book did I reflect more deeply, even spiritually, on how privileged bodies—be the privilege whiteness, wealth, masculinity, Christianity, heterosexuality, or a cisgender identity—define safety and threats. What personal stories have provoked people in positions of systemic power to call for police assistance and protection against marginalized citizens whose eating, sleeping, walking, jogging, playing, praying, or working is perceived to disrupt their safety? Subconscious triggers from personal stories in the lives of white law enforcement, for example, converted responses to nonviolent calls into use-of-deadly-force tragedies. Why are a disproportionate number of Black folks dying as compared to white folks when we review data of loss of civilian life during interactions with police?[1]

In 2014, Dylann Roof, a white man, killed nine people at a church, was apprehended with no physical harm, and received a meal from a fast-food restaurant following his arrest for racially motivated crimes he admitted to doing. Then in 2020, George Floyd, a Black man, was reported to law enforcement by a store clerk for allegedly passing a counterfeit $20 bill and was publicly choked and suffocated to death by a police officer with a street full of eyewitnesses. Optics from police behavior might suggest Dylann Roof was less threatening to police officers. What made Dylann Roof feel safer to law enforcement than Trayvon Martin in 2012? Or Michael Brown in 2014? Or Tyre King in 2016? Or Henry Green in 2016? Or George Floyd in 2020? Or Casey Goodson in 2020? Or Andre Hill in 2020?

The difference in incidents between law enforcement and white folks versus law enforcement and Black and Brown folks is about one's personal perception of safety and threat. What we will never know are the details of the tiny, subconscious, implicit grains of memories in each law enforcement person's mind who impulsively felt unsafe when she or he pulled the trigger a bit too quickly. What we struggle to control is how our bodies and minds partner to keep us safe when we feel threatened—or how far they will go to keep us safe and alive. What if, because we are not in relationships with one another and we do not know one another, folks with the least amount of privilege and power are perceived to be threats to the safety and well-being of folks with the most privilege and power? And what if the folks with the most privilege and power also have greater access to lead our schools, churches, first response organizations, business industries, and elected political offices? What happens to the safety of othered people if the most powerful people understand, and trust, them the least?

While this book is not specifically about racial injustice and systemic oppression, it is about human beings and human systems and about how we can do a better job at practicing true humanity. Who of us has not experienced a trauma or deeply distressing experience? It can be difficult to navigate through the most difficult moments of our lives and emerge better, stronger, and more loving than before. That is, however, exactly what is required of us to do no harm, or at least less harm, to others. If hurt people hurt people, then healed people can heal people. The Nine Asks is more than a list of conversation guidelines. It implores us to dig deeper into who we were, who we are, and who we want to be. The Nine Asks is an invitation to those with the greatest access to safety from those with less or the very least access to safety to see and honor the humanity, existence, and needs of those whose voices, identities, and lives have been othered, marginalized, and disenfranchised. The stories in this book call us to question when we have sacrificed the safety of others to feel more secure. More than the Nine Asks, there is one constant ask we must consider when weighing our safety needs against those of others: Do I care enough about you to take up less space with my needs and make more room for yours? If your answer is yes, thank you for responding to the most critical ask and accepting the most fundamental invitation. Caring enough to change makes change possible.

An "Invitation" to the Asks

Words and manners matter. Being *told* to participate as opposed to *invited* into fellowship changes how we engage a space. Think about an experience you've had at work or in the classroom when a person in a position of power over the space (a supervisor, teacher, parent, etc.) told you an activity was mandatory. Requiring or mandating meaningful human engagement is a kiss of death. It's a sure way to expect people to close off instead of open up. Telling someone to engage and be personal is like telling someone to feel. If one cannot choose whether to participate or not, then one of the only things they have power over is the management of their thoughts, feelings, and words in the moment. Hence, the result is often, "You can make me attend, but you can't make me talk," and "If you force me to talk, you can't make me feel or care." It is not uncommon for us to be open and receptive to an experience *until* we are told our participation is required. Once the element of choice is removed, it negatively impacts our ability to be open, willing, honest, and vulnerable.

"We're going to talk" feels a lot less safe than "Can we talk?" "Would you be open to talking?" is even better. "Do you have the capacity to talk?" is most ideal in extending the invitation for connection as it also asks the individual to consider their desire, availability, and emotional readiness for conversation. Invitations can be accepted or declined. The invitee chooses their level of engagement.

There is a reason why it is called the Nine Asks as opposed to the Nine Directives. There is intent behind the framework being referenced as an invitation, not orders. When others are asked to share personal information and stories about themselves under the auspice of directives and guidelines, power differential has entered the equation. Directions, instructions, and guidelines might suggest there is a right or wrong way for you to be who you are. Whether, when, how, why, where, and with whom one wants to be involved matters in crafting a space safe enough for the Nine Asks and especially Ask #1 to manifest. In part 2, we'll be exploring each of the Nine Asks. Reflecting on all that you've just learned about safety and trauma, note that it's important to invite people into practicing the Asks—not ordering them to follow rules of conversational engagement. By removing the element of control over people and situations and not obstructing people in accessing their own power to choose, it is communicated and understood that the space desires to be safer.

PART TWO
THE NINE ASKS

THE NINE ASKS: Safer Space Invitations
"I ask that you ..."

1. Be as Honest and Vulnerable as Possible.

The goal of a Nine Asks community of practice is for participants be as close to our whole selves as possible while in the presence and fellowship of others. In efforts to reciprocate authenticity during conversation, don't tell me what you think I want to hear. Tell me the truth about what you think, how you feel, and who you really are. Dig a little deeper than transactional conversation.

2. Respect Boundaries and Thresholds.

There may be times when dialogue uncovers pain I do not desire to share or relive in a practice community. While being ever vigilant of working toward stretching ourselves, respect every individual's right and discretion to avoid disclosure to the point of being put in harm's way.

3. Practice No Judgment.

When I agree to participate in a practice community, I understand that the format invites participants to process different identity and affinity lenses through personal experiences. Because perception is reality, my experiences are not "wrong"—just different. Work to treat the differences as opportunities to learn about perspectives alternative to your own.

4. Honor Confidentiality.

When you talk with people outside of our community, honor the fact that I expressly own my own narrative. Honor my agency and discretion to choose when, where, how, through whom, and what part of my story can be re-shared (or not) outside of a practice community. That includes my name and identity markers.

5. Come Back to Me.

Trust that I am making every effort to engage in an honest and appreciative dialogue in a practice community. There is diversity in the temperaments of information processors in a practice community (introverts, extroverts, etc.), and at times, I need a moment to prepare my thoughts and responses before sharing. This may require a little patience from both of us and the acknowledgment that (my) silence is also a voice.

6. Respect the Process of Learning the "Right" Language.

There will absolutely be times when you or I contribute to the conversation, and the words/mannerisms may not be expressed in the most affirming manner. Know that I am approaching the process and the topic of discussion with the best of intentions. Let's commit to accept each other *where we are* and, if possible, help each other in the process of reframing thoughts to be more accurate and affirming.

7. Take the Time to Listen First.

Sometimes in conversation—particularly ones in which we are passionately engaged—we may take a turn to speak instead of actively listening. Try to listen to me completely and then determine if a response is warranted or welcomed. When we yield to each other in dialogue, it maximizes the capacity for inclusion of *everyone's* voices.

8. Grant Permission to Go Deeper or Decline.

Every conversation should be treated as a teachable moment when we can be both students *and* teachers. When I am a student, I reserve the right to ask questions in an effort to deepen the conversation and gain information that will help broaden my perspective. When I am a teacher, I reserve the right to decline answering questions if the inquiry poses a threat—whether perceived or real—to my boundaries and thresholds. Asking is allowed, and no is an acceptable answer.

9. Stay in Your Seat.

During passionate conversations, it is natural to have verbal as well as nonverbal reactions. Make thorough attempts to notice the body language and unspoken cues of those around you. Show up and be present even if you anticipate the dialogue will be difficult. Stay connected and see the conversation through while communicating in a way that is not verbally, physically, or emotionally threatening to others.

CHAPTER 3

Ask #1
Be as Honest and Vulnerable as Possible

Think about how many transactional and surface-level conversations we have on a daily basis. Some of us are so desperate to avoid having conversation of any depth, meaning, or value that we isolate ourselves and avoid human contact even in public places. Have you ever taken the stairs to avoid riding in an elevator with others? Do you make a beeline for the self-checkout lane in grocery stores to avoid trivial conversation? Have you ever hoped your potential plane or train seat neighbor misses their trip so that you can travel alone in peace? If you said yes to any of these questions, don't feel bad. You're not cruel; you're human. How curious it is that humans have been designed to be social creatures, and yet, more often than not, we do everything in our power to avoid human interaction?

Ask #1 is to be as honest and vulnerable as possible. Of the Nine Asks, the request for people in human systems to be transparent and ready themselves for real conversations is paramount. This is arguably the most important Ask. If we don't get Ask #1 correct, the other Asks do not matter and are not possible. Ask #1 sets the tone for the conversation. It is the entry point into the invitation for authentic human engagement.

Red Light: What to Stop, Look, and Listen For

Meaningful conversation does not have to be operationalized or micromanaged. And it doesn't have to be weird. Human beings and our stories are fascinating all by themselves. Make room for people to blossom, especially if we desire to genuinely connect with others, and let simple connection be enough. It can be a stretch to push past our discomfort. In fact, in many cultures—including and especially in US culture—deeper, non-surface-level conversations can be perceived as awkward and abnormal. The practice of Ask #1 battles a general and ongoing resistance to feel our feelings and to expose our feelings to others. Might any of the following roadblocks be in your way of practicing Ask #1?

We don't want to feel our own feelings. For some, deep feelings—especially if they are distressing—are not to be revisited. We may know that emotions exist underneath the surface, but we may experience apprehension in sitting still in the feelings. It is easier to be transactional. It is simpler to get the work done without human relationships. However, suppression of emotion over time can make us sick. Although our feelings may not be comfortable or pleasurable all the time, allowing them to be felt and released is key to holistic wellness.

We don't trust people with our emotions. If I do not trust myself with my own emotions, then I most certainly will not trust anyone else with them either. Some people have had sincere disappointments after trusting that a person was a safe space for them to share, only to find out the person did not have capacity to be a worthy recipient of their thoughts and feelings. While we have rights and reasons for why we may not trust certain individuals with our thoughts, feelings, and emotions, it ultimately hurts only us in the end if we never make any attempts to trust anyone with anything. Humans are designed to be social.

We fear falling apart and not being able to pull ourselves back together. Many folks are afraid of losing control should they express their emotions and then not being able to regain control. The good news is that our bodies are designed to heal themselves when we are hurt. We have the potential for our brain functions to recalibrate after emotional moments. And what if the parts of us that we are worrying about losing need to fall away or shed for us to grow?

We don't want to feel weak or dysfunctional. The desire to be strong in appearance is one that many can understand. This false sense of strength and security is especially prevalent in BIPOC (Black, Indigenous and People of Color) communities and especially among women in racialized non-white bodies. The laws of nature teach in very explicit ways that harm and even extinction can be the results of weakness and dysfunction. It is in our best interest, we believe, to appear as healthy and strong as possible. However, no one is strong all the time.

We don't want to feel unrelatable. In our original states, none of us desired to be outcasts. In fact, in our early days, our safety was incumbent on us fitting in with the group. Standing out was dangerous. Sometimes standing out and being perceived as othered *is* dangerous. When we have the experience of being unrelatable, it can feel isolating.

We don't like feeling helpless, needy, and incapable of taking care of our problems. Helplessness — whether real or perceived — can feel petrifying. Sometimes opening up to reveal your deepest, darkest secrets also exposes one's ineptness. For most, there is a comfort in feeling as if things are under control. Unfortunately, sometimes we just aren't OK. Sometimes we need help to become regulated, rebalanced, and stabilized. It is not possible for us to do it all on our own.

We are in the practice of supporting others but not being supported. Caregivers, go-to people, and leaders tend to have difficulty opening up and being vulnerable because we are simply out of practice. We don't ask for help; we supply the help. We are very rarely checked on by others, though we make it our business to ensure the needs of everyone else are being met. If you are not in the practice of being checked on and taken care of, not being open or vulnerable may be a manifestation of not being *asked* to be open and vulnerable over time. Giving others our talents, time, and treasures is principally a good thing. However, if we condition ourselves and others to expect us to only give and never receive help and support, then extreme caregiving can become a liability to our personal wellness. Unfortunately, we can train ourselves and others that our stories and needs are not important enough to share in comparison to others.

We fear our emotions will be weaponized against us. Heaven forbid we open up and get vulnerable with the wrong person, only to have said individual use our words or actions against us. The experience of betrayal, harm, and manipulation is a paralyzing hurt. When the tension goes beyond mistrust and transitions into threat, the five *f*'s (fight, flight, freeze, fawn, and flock) kick in. Trauma triggers activate our mind's best attempts at implementing coping strategies to save and protect us when a perceived threat presents itself. Trauma elicits five emotional responses which we cannot prevent or control:

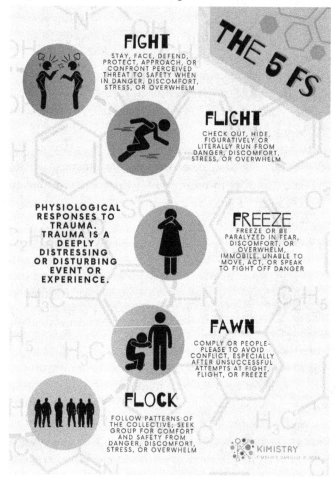

Fight: Confront the threat
Flight: Run away from the threat
Freeze: Get stuck when facing the threat
Fawn: Give in or give up to the threat
Flock: Follow group action amid the threat

The five *f*'s are physiological responses to trauma, and when activated, they send us on an emotional and behavioral cycle that is difficult to interrupt. Our brains do what they must for our perceived protection. For some, protection means never again opening up or trusting anyone with our thoughts and feelings.

We don't want to be associated with stigmas and stereotypes. Although there is no such thing as normal, in so many ways, we try to have a semblance of a normal life. The perception of normal is what is most widely accepted and, therefore, protected and kept safe. The admittance that we are slightly adjacent to or, for some, far from normal can be a very dysregulating feeling. Abnormal identity and behavior are almost invariably stigmatized and stereotyped. Humanity has a well-documented record demonstrating risk for a life of lower quality or harm when stigmatized and stereotyped.

We don't know how to go deeper, or there's nothing deeper to access. Though there is often more to an individual than meets the eye, most do not dig deeper and search for reasons why they feel how they feel or do the things that they do. Many accept their thoughts, feelings, and behaviors at face value and believe that there is not a more substantive cause. They might just believe that "it is what it is and it ain't what it ain't."

Yellow Light: Proceed to Practice with Caution

Practicing Ask #1 has one major ingredient: trust. Before going any further, it must be boldly and clearly stated that no one owes us anything—including their trust. We have not automatically earned folks' confidence in us, and subsequently we do not automatically earn folks' stories. There is an opportunity to earn trust in every moment and in every interaction. Without trust, there are no safer, braver spaces. Without trust, there is no value in the Nine Asks.

The routinely displayed effort of earning trust is the linchpin to all functional relationships in human systems. Once we earn trust, we can attempt to be honest and vulnerable with other people. But how do we practice the virtue of gaining others' trust on a granular level?

Practice Example: "Open Hands, Open Hearts"
After the third disturbingly emotional prayer service in a month, Abby, the committee chair of the women's ministry, invited a special guest to present on trauma and healing. Abby introduced Deidre, the speaker, with a personal testimony of their work together, and Deidre made her way to the podium, welcomed by cordial smiles and golf claps. The attendees were prepared to tune out, when the speaker got their attention by going against protocol and asking, "Is it OK if I come closer to you and don't stand behind the podium?" The crowd cautiously nodded in approval. "Squeeze your hands in a tight fist," Deidre requested of the attendees as she walked to the center of the room. The women acquiesced as sixty seconds ticked by. Noticing their growing discomfort, she explained, "Some of you want blessings and gifts placed in your palms, but you can't receive them if your hands are clenched shut." A few of the women sat up in their seats. She then asked the group how they were doing but called for them to answer by reflecting on how their bodies felt. Brows furrowed and lips bunched, twisted, and pulled to one side. They had not considered any links between their dispositions and physical states.

Deidre asked again, "Where do you feel the stress of the last few months in your *body*?" She scanned the room and made eye contact with the women. As they touched their bodies and mumbled, she affirmed them and called out their responses. "Yes, your shoulders," to a woman in the front. "Your back, mm-hmm," to a church mother near the exit door. "You feel it in your head? Sure," she affirmed to a younger woman near the refreshments table. "Ah, your chest. Yes," she acknowledged to another in the rear. Deidre inquired further and asked if anyone experienced strange body aches with no medical diagnoses. More raised their hands. She then asked about how folks were sleeping. As she prompted them, looking at the women and talking to them directly, they softened and began conversing with her. Deidre then confessed about how stress and trauma had impacted her respiratory system and led to her treatment for skin disorders and insomnia.

The women viscerally reacted. Some froze; others stirred in their seats. Most were uncomfortable with the vulnerability, but all were fully attentive. She carefully balanced information dissemination on physiological manifestations of stress and inheritable trauma with responses to their inquiries. When the room felt tight with emotion, she made space for it by either pausing or verbally acknowledging the tension and discomfort she sensed among them. In moments when she recognized the room needed bravery, she offered tender narratives from her own life and family. When she made room for compassion, they inched closer to her energetically. The more she offered, the more the women shared. The deeper she divulged in content, the further the women sought to go in their revealing—eventually in both verbal and written formats. Some spoke with trembling voices. Others shed tears silently in their seats. By the end of the event, the women prayed over one another, talked in small groups, and waited for individual time to hug and chat with Deidre privately.

What happened from the start to the end of this women's ministry meeting that shifted the mood of the room? The answer is Ask #1. Was Deidre a phenomenal orator? Not necessarily. However, Deidre knew that Ask #1 and its implementation of honesty and vulnerability would be the dealmaker or deal-breaker in gaining trust and connectivity with the women. She applied several elements in her practice of Ask #1 that sped up the process of rapport building. Let's examine how she did it.

Beginning the practice of Ask #1 can be rough and rocky. Deidre recognized that although the women chose to come to the meeting, they were emotionally guarded. She used multiple conversation prompts as opportunities to invite the participants to engage in dialogue with her (and even with one another). Sometimes the spirit or energy between people speaks at a much higher volume than verbal language. These moments require us to pay emotional attention to the presence of nonverbal cues. Deidre acknowledged the subject matter was difficult. She paused when she noticed their faces and bodies were communicating messages that words could not convey. She respected their depleted capacity and allowed the room to adjust when vulnerability felt heavy.

Sawubona is a South African term from the Zulu culture. Its translation means, "I see you." This meaning is deeper than literal optics of visually seeing a person. It involves feeling and receiving the human existence and the beingness of the person in front of you. The response to Sawubona is Shikoba. *Shikoba* means, "I am here." The relationship between Sawubona and Shikoba means, "Before you saw me, I did not exist." The practice of Sawubona and Shikoba is to make people feel visible and seen in a deeper way. Deidre repeatedly conveyed to the women that she saw them, desired to honor their whole existence, and wanted to hear their real stories.

Repeating back dialogue to a storyteller is another way to demonstrate active listening and mindful presence. Deidre repeated back descriptions the women used to communicate their physical aches and pains. Then when the conversation grew personal, she attempted to share what she perceived as the intention and emotion behind their words and gestures. "When you shared _____, I felt _____." In doing so, she demonstrated the impact and value of their vulnerable stories on her. Deidre listened curiously and affirmed their bravery. There was no pressure to share *anything*, nor was there pressure to share *everything*. Some storytellers were just brave enough to tell the truth. A few storytellers were ready to be both honest and vulnerable about their emotional battles. Regardless of the level of depth, whenever someone spoke up, Deidre simply looked them in the eyes and replied, "Thank you for sharing." A statement of appreciation and affirmation can go a long way. She let them know how amazing they were for pushing past fear and being brave enough to explore sensitivity in the truths of their stories. She modeled that sharing stories can change lives and speak truth to power.

Green Light: Go Forth and Be Great

Being honest and vulnerable is hard and emotional. It is perfectly understandable that asking people to bare their souls (or at least their authenticity) is a tough request to extend to others. Sometimes deep discussions make challenging thoughts feel more real. It might evoke frustration to find words to accurately match feelings. For those who have experienced deeper hurts, harms, and traumas, the telling of stories and narratives can stir up emotional currents that feel dangerous. Sometimes it evokes anger and tears. Saying a brave thing aloud may unlock discomfort and apprehensions folks don't realize they have or even fears they thought had been conquered but, in fact, have never truly subsided. Sometimes it takes real conversation to understand ourselves and to be understood by others.

Ask #1 does not require folks to be fearless in compassionately engaging with others; it asks us to do it afraid. Asking or telling someone to be unafraid can sound insensitive and may diminish the involuntary but very real somatic and physiological experience of our feelings of fear. We may not choose to be angry, nervous, sad, uncomfortable, or threatened; however, logic, reasoning, and others' (good) intentions don't change the reality when we feel heavy feelings. Instead of urging folks to be fearless, Ask #1 implores us to stretch ourselves to be a little braver when we are invited to gift a piece of ourselves to someone.

One of the most humbling and beautiful experiences is bearing witness to human beings who fight through fear to find their voices and share their stories. Sure, there is much at stake when weighing the pros and cons of being vulnerable *or not*. The good news is that in a safer, braver, and more courageous space, there are rewards for the risk of being vulnerable. The invitation to be open and transparent is less common than we might imagine. So many of us have innumerable examples of an awareness or belief that, "Nobody cares, nor do they want to hear the truth." Imagine, then, the phenomenon of folks coming together as strangers, contributing to the co-design and co-creation of a safer, braver, and more courageous space, and being transformed by the experience. Consider what a cathartic surprise it might be for a person to have no expectation of engagement or connection with anyone and then to feel seen by the exhibited compassion of a stranger. (Even people with whom we are familiar may essentially be strangers until we accept the opportunity to connect on a personal or deeper level.) Creating relationships, connection, and familiarity is an invaluable gift we can give to others all the time. Our reward is earning trust and, subsequently, one's authentic voice and story.

So much sensitivity surrounds our stories. They are deeply personal. Ask #1 is not requesting for people to bleed out their stories and divulge all their personal business. The DNA of our stories includes the emotional equity of every experience we have ever had. Each reflection and memory, whether shared or sitting silent in our souls, has connections to arguably inexplicable feelings that are not necessarily ready to be offered for the consumption of others. For some, vulnerability feels volatile. It requires an incredible amount of empathy and compassion to be a worthy recipient of someone's story and voice. Sometimes we are not aware of the live, ungrounded wires in our stories: parts and pieces of loose and, at times, dangerous energy that has not yet been properly channeled. It is imperative that every story told be managed with the utmost care.

We are all worthy of being seen. Making someone feel seen and allowing their stories to be truly heard also brings transparency and awareness of their gifts, talents, abilities, strengths, and anointing. I have been humbled and grateful to be entrusted with stories of human perseverance, resilience, survival, grit, and personification of miracles. Some of my emergent teachers buried children, were formerly incarcerated, live with HIV and AIDS, battle mental health and mood disorders, immigrated from refugee camps, survived horrific abuse, and more. While these are harrowing tales, the vulnerability also shown a spotlight on their amazing grace. In speaking their truths, they began to recognize the tone, tenor, and melody of their memoirs.

Through regular practice and eventual embodiment of Ask #1, flat and transactional information can transform into manifested empathy, care, and compassion. Like Deidre, we can support people feeling seen, heard, valued, and appreciated. We can reverse doubt that we don't want and that we can't handle honesty. We can convince others that they are worthy of an audience and that their stories matter. The next time an opportunity presents itself to either listen or share sincerely, earnestly, and genuinely, embrace it! Hold the space. Be present in mind, body, and spirit. Imagine open hands and the precious gift of a voice being placed inside. Vow to let nothing happen to the gift. Hold the space and embrace the moment. We are ready.

CHAPTER 4

Ask #2
Respect Boundaries and Thresholds

Ask #2 is a request to respect boundaries and thresholds. This Ask is special in that it is a simultaneous request for all persons in human engagement, irrespective of who is talking, listening, or even observing conversation. It calls for every person connected to said scenario in human engagement to notice the condition and role of their bodies before, during, and after dialogue. Whether you are the person taking the risk by stretching and sharing when you talk or whether you are the person tempering yourself to actively listen when you would like to speak, your body is having a conversation with you. It's letting you know when the conversation is going well and when the conversation might take a turn for the worse and bring you discomfort. The discomfort could show up expressively as confusion, sadness, guilt, anger, or many other emotions. This is the tipping point in conversation before the mental shutdown occurs and likely the last moment you will have control over your emotional responses before your brain and body partner together to take over. Once your brain believes you are not safe in the conversation, it will respond and try to "save" you, whether you like it or not. Our heads can lie to us. Our hearts often lie to us. Our bodies never lie. Ask #2 insists that, in conversation, our bodies are telling us when we are or are not OK to navigate dialogue (capacity), what we need to do to take care of and protect ourselves (boundaries), and how much we can take before we perceive that a line has been crossed (thresholds).

For better or worse, children are the most liberated in instinctively responding to their bodies. We have all seen a child have a behavioral meltdown in a public space with an exasperated adult. Those moments, albeit embarrassing for the parents or guardians, are truthful responses and are the results of a human who has reached and likely exceeded their threshold of what they can handle. The mind told the body to shut down, and the body was obedient. As we get older, wiser, and more disciplined, we ideally develop better external control over our demonstrated emotions. Yet just because we "calmed down," "fixed our faces," or "watched our mouths" does not mean that the heightened feelings dissipated. Societal norms will not permit us as adults to release emotion in the form of a temper tantrum without coarse judgment and consequences. If said behavior was acceptable, there would be many more emotionally regulated adults! In the absence of letting it all go in the middle of running errands or work meetings when boundaries and thresholds have been besieged, the work of Ask #2 is relegated to mindfulness practices.

Red Light: What to Stop, Look, and Listen For

Ask #2 is a request to respect boundaries and thresholds. However, fear and discomfort disrupt language, comprehension, conversation, and connection. Once fear is activated, it is like switching the control panel to autopilot. We are no longer in charge or in control once we become upset. Feelings and emotions can become huge distractions to logic and reasoning. Dr. Dan Siegel, clinical professor of psychiatry at the UCLA School of Medicine and executive director of the Mindsight Institute, is the creator of a useful framework for understanding how emotions work in our brains. He calls his theory "flipping your lid," and it demonstrates what happens when we transition from our thinking brain to our feeling brain. In other words, this explanation may help us understand what happens when boundaries and thresholds are violated and we "lose our cool" or composure in conversation.

Let's make a hand model of the brain. Hold up your hand like you are making a fist with your thumb tucked under your four fingers. Imagine this is your brain. The back of your hand, which flows down to your wrist, is the back of your head including the back of your brain and your brain stem. Your face is on the finger side, with your knuckles representing where your forehead is. When we feel calm, secure, and safe, our core feelings are protected just as our fingers are tightly protecting our thumb. This experience is what is generally understood as being *regulated*. In this state, there is the highest likelihood that we can access the area of our brain where executive functioning lives. This area—the frontal cortex—is where logical and intellectual thoughts reside, including attention, reasoning, judgment, problem solving, creativity, emotional regulation, impulse control, and awareness of self and others. In great, stimulating, affirming, and healthy conversations, our thoughts and brain activity will ideally ping in this area.

However, when we are dysregulated, our energy and brain activity leave the sweet spot of the frontal cortex and begin traveling lower in the brain. The more dysregulated we are, the higher the likelihood that the activity takes a pit stop in our amygdala—and this is not-so-great news. In the amygdala, our feelings and impulses tell our brains something is wrong. This raises our awareness or "flips our lid." Imagine the four fingers now standing up straight, exposing our thumb. The thumb represents the amygdala, and this area of the brain is where irrationality lives. The amygdala is home to anxiety, aggression, fear conditioning, emotional memory, and social cognition. When we are dysregulated, our raw emotions are exposed, and our boundaries and thresholds have effectively been breached.

A great deal of (over)stimulation could show up in your mind and body during the practice of Ask #2. Calming down before reaching your escalation point is key. Reflect on these questions in a moment of solitude and stillness to better understand your existing boundaries and thresholds:

How much time do you have before you burst? The truth is, as adults, we wait too long to notice and admit when we are uncomfortable. If we notice the discomfort, we often do not react in a timely matter. We convince ourselves that we are not upset or that we can suppress our emotions and deal with it later. There is a window of opportunity to ground and regulate when feelings and emotions exceed capacity. If we miss that window and if we do not release the energy in a healthy and effective way, we are at risk of time working against us and of the energy turning into sickness in our bodies and minds.

What is your body telling you? The less we know the stories of our bodies, the less capable we are of taking care of ourselves in deep and meaningful ways. Whether we want to admit it or not, physiological manifestations of stress, trauma, and harm are part of the human experience. There is a way you react unconsciously and somatically when you feel unsafe or uncomfortable. In the absence of understanding what your body does when you are upset, you miss early warning signs alerting you that you need grounding, consciousness, and care.

Do you know what your triggers are? It is not uncommon for someone to downplay what bothers and disrupts them. It is taboo to appear sensitive. Humans from all walks of life respect having "thicker skin." Nevertheless, while trying to be tough and save face, we may be at risk of both suffering at the hands of the external threat as well as becoming a threat to our own emotional safety. When we do not know or fail to admit what topics and issues hurt or upset us in conversation, we put ourselves in harm's way—whether intentionally or unintentionally. The threat to safety, then, prowls internally as well as externally.

What's "too far" and "too much" for you? In most instances with the Nine Asks and especially with Ask #2, application of our needs as givers and receivers is person specific. This book began with an invitation to consider that our understanding of safety and threats are individual and inextricably linked to our personal stories, histories, and experiences. Therefore, a boundary for you is likely not a boundary for me. And your threshold is almost guaranteed to be different than mine. Though it sounds fair and equitable as a practice, a common group boundary and threshold may not be possible or effective to establish.

Yellow Light: Proceed to Practice with Caution

When we become fearful, unsafe, or uncomfortable in human engagement, the amygdala takes over in increasing chances for emotional outburst or overwhelm us. Attention shifts from focusing on others to my mind focusing on *me* and *my* feelings. And because bodies and minds are at work whether we are speaking, listening, or observing, tense and dynamic human engagement could result in a space filled with dysregulated people and contagious hypervigilance in one fell swoop. We bring old wounds into new experiences. Others are unaware when conversation topics or methods pour salt into an open sore. Moreover, sometimes we are unaware that an emotional wound has not healed until it is mishandled in engagement with others.

Practice Example: "The Eruption of Mount Dee-Dee"
For the last two decades, buried emotions and a lack of healthy self-care practices plagued Dee-Dee. Family dysfunction was at the root, especially regarding the strained relationship with her mother, Louisa. Instead of leaning into her private healing journey, she chose a career path providing public service to others as a case manager for a human services agency. She had a stellar career over the years and was rewarded for commendable workplace acumen with promotion after promotion. Outside of work, she was an active volunteer for worthy causes, and she took pride in being her inner circle's dependable friend and "mama bear." Everyone praised Dee-Dee's dedication and commitment. She accepted calls for help day and night. She checked her email and text messages constantly. Dee-Dee had no boundaries when it came to caregiving. However, she was very private about her family dysfunction and often avoided conversation about her mother. Dee-Dee claimed that service was her self-care. Eventually, her constant service and virtuous deeds resulted in her being personally shut down, closed off, disengaged, and disconnected from friends, family, and even her own feelings and needs.

Dee-Dee had perfected caregiving for others to the extent that she could no longer gauge when she was near, at, or beyond capacity—both physically and emotionally. Her unmet needs began to look and feel like self-inflicted punishment, which manifested in the form of anxiety and depression. She did not know when "enough was enough" nor how to protect herself from feeling overwhelmed. One afternoon when Dee-Dee was completely exhausted, a colleague made a taxing request and Dee-Dee confessed that she could not honor the ask. Caught off guard by the decline, the colleague made a thoughtless joke about Dee-Dee and her relationship with her mother, Louisa. The joke unexpectedly triggered Dee-Dee. Usually, she buckled under her colleague's combat, having lost so many arguments before. This time, her conflict avoidance proved to be futile as well. A line was crossed. Dee-Dee's cheeks tingled. The back of her neck warmed as her body temperature increased. Her stomach filled with butterflies, and her eyes welled with tears of anger. Before Dee-Dee knew it, she unmuted, unfroze, and unleashed an explosion of repressed emotions in her colleague's direction. Her blazing retort ended the battle and all future irreverent commentary. Unfortunately, it also resulted in both Dee-Dee and her colleague being physically unwell that evening and becoming unsafe spaces for each other moving forward.

What went wrong during Dee-Dee and her colleague's conversation? The answer is a kerfuffle of Ask #2. Both individuals missed or misread their boundaries and thresholds. There were signs that the dialogue was transitioning from bad to worse. Both could have walked away from, ended, or changed the conversation at any point. However, they kept going when their bodies, minds, and spirits urgently expressed that they were headed for disaster. Dee-Dee's body tried to flag her down that it needed some emergency self-care. It knew she was beyond the capacity of what she could handle and be well. Psychiatrist, author, researcher, and educator Bessel van der Kolk penned *The Body Keeps the Score*, which revolutionized wellness by providing empirical research on trauma and somatics (experiences of the body). According to van der Kolk, when we feel fear or discomfort, there is a transference of emotional experiences into our physical bodies. More simply stated, there is a reason why headaches, high blood pressure, digestive issues, dermatological issues, and other health challenges often follow stress, burnout, hurt, anger, or overwhelm. Negative feelings don't just go away. When our boundaries and thresholds are violated, the absence of felt safety roots in our bodies. Left untreated and unaddressed, this can lead to a myriad of physical, social, mental, and spiritual challenges that get in the way of us experiencing safety, bravery and courage in the company of others. Dee-Dee felt unsafe, shut down, and eventually shattered her silence because trauma was still in her body. Dee-Dee didn't "go crazy" or "lose it." She got stuck in the Misfit Matrix, a pattern that emerges in communication when we have not done the work of healing from old hurts and traumas.

The Misfit Matrix
Fitting in gives access to safety and security within a group. Even in the animal kingdom, there is safety in being a part of the pack as opposed to running the risk of trying to survive alone. Humans experience the same thing. The feeling of acceptance, belongingness, and fitting in with a human system (e.g., school, work, church, friends, or family) is easier for some than others. Those whose identities and interests are in alignment with what is considered normal tend to fit in more easily. Unfortunately, when someone stands out or apart from environmental or societal norms, they may feel, be perceived as, or even be definitively labeled a misfit. Whether folks are easily recognized misfits or whether they culturally code-switch (adjust behavior, appearance, speech, etc. to conform with the social norms of an environment) to hide their true identity, misfits have very different experiences within human systems from those who fit in naturally.

The Misfit Matrix concept has four stages. *Stage 1* begins with a traumatic or emotionally distressing experience (Dee-Dee's family trauma). *Stage 2* of the matrix happens after one survives the trauma and is in a new scenario or experience. Though the trauma is in the past, said person may be hypervigilant and have heightened awareness about perceived threats that remind them of people, places, things, or ideas which were previously a threat or caused harm (Dee-Dee's caregiving was a way of shutting down connection to her own feelings and needs).

In *stage 3*, following fear, there is a change in behavior because protection is the preeminent goal. When fear surfaces, the five *f*'s are activated, and one is no longer able to fully engage in logical and rational thinking. Instead, the person (re)enters survival mode. Dee-Dee cycled through the five *f*'s, and her brain chose to fight. When the five *f*'s are initiated, Ask #2 — to respect the boundaries and thresholds of others — goes out the window. By *stage 4*, said individual is no longer engaged with or interested in connecting with people in an environment (Dee-Dee disengaged from her family and her colleague).

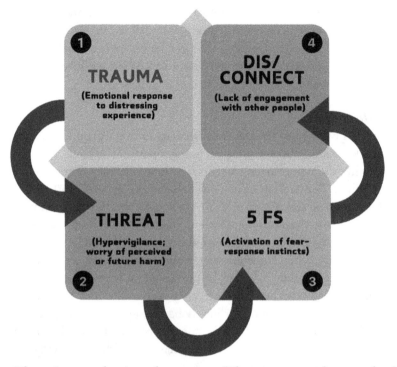

There is an aphorism that states, "If you stay ready, you don't have to get ready." Self-care is the best measure for respecting our boundaries and thresholds. (Special note for caregivers: service is not self-care!) If only Dee-Dee would have been in the practice of taking better care of herself. Four strongly suggested items for your self-care toolkit include:

1. *Creating a personal safety plan.* In moments when our efforts are futile and when the environments are volatile or threatening, establish an *internal* safety plan. Reflect on what makes you feel whole. Think about and do things that make you feel safe. Round up your circle of trusted advisors and confidantes. If necessary, prepare your escape plan when you begin to reach capacity. Notice when you are close to your breaking point and take that as a sign to reach for your own oxygen mask.

2. *Incorporating an internal locus of control.* American psychologist Julian B. Rotter developed a concept called *locus of control* that addresses beliefs about behaviors having control over

outcomes. Internal locus of control means we believe our circumstances are impacted by our own behaviors as opposed to the behaviors of others (external locus of control). Don't expend disproportionate amounts of energy trying to change people, places, things, ideas, and circumstances that are impossible for you to change. Take care of yourself! Focus on changing how you react and respond to things that make you uncomfortable.

3. *Practicing regulation strategies, especially in tough conversations.* When we have reached our limit, we often try to do the head and heart work first and the body work second. However, deeper thinking requires us to be regulated, and when we are upset, we are *not* regulated. When you feel yourself reaching the limits of your boundaries and thresholds, calm your body down. Drink water. Take a walk. Practice breathing techniques. Hold and hug yourself. Learn how to do emotional freedom techniques (also known as tapping). Take a nap. Cry, dance, sing, or write. Find some relief to calm your body down to make room for reflection and deeper thinking.

4. *Guarding your heart and bracing for the pain.* When the worst-case scenario is reality and when the impairment of our comfort, harmony, and courage is inevitable, practice extending yourself radical grace. Surround yourself with people who you are certain love and care about you. Speak kind affirmations over yourself. Pray and meditate for protection if prayer is part of your lifestyle. When pain is an inevitability, ready yourself with realistic expectations and a plan for triage.

Green Light: Go Forth and Be Great

Glorious light exists at the end of the tunnel when we get Ask #2 right. Solid practice can result in us becoming all-around holistically better human beings. When you are in the practice of having greater compassion for yourself, compassion becomes contagious. It will become easier to take others' needs into consideration and to take better care of others. Once you have a profound understanding of the physiological impacts of words and deeds, it should become difficult to speak harshly to others. Ask #2 strengthens our practice of empathy toward others. There is fragility in being human. We are at war with ourselves and others constantly. Life is hard. We all benefit from a continual exchange of unearned favor and the gifts of acceptance, grace, and forgiveness. The miracle of our fearful and wonderful neurobiological craftmanship is that we really can change. Our brains are pliable, meaning that they can take new form and shape. We are not locked into our old thinking. It is possible scientifically and spiritually to have a renewed mind.

For some, when we survive something challenging, we bury it deep with the hope we will never have to touch or confront it again. Like our friend Dee-Dee, though, when we least expect it, our old baggage has a way of showing up. If we haven't visited our weaknesses, shortcomings, and secret hurts in a while, Ask #2 invites us into our shadow work. It is not possible to respect boundaries and thresholds with excellence while avoiding our deeper idiosyncrasies and proclivities. To be human is to have baggage. There is *something* that bothers you. There is *something* you don't want to hear or don't want to talk about. Most folks have a "red button" they do not want anyone to push. This Ask requires you to have an intimate idea of what those matters are, how they got there, why they bother you, and what you ultimately need to mitigate the discomfort that comes when the proverbial buttons are pushed. There is nothing like walking in the weeds of someone else's overgrown garden to remind us that we need to do some weeding of our own. One of the best ways we can love and serve others is to ensure our stuff does not get in the way when connection is possible. Go to therapy. Get a (life) coach. Forgive someone or yourself. Journal. Get a checkup with your wellness professional. Mend a severed relationship. Do your own healing work. Do it early and often.

Ask #2 explains the mental and physical triggers we feel during passionate dialogue and requires regular mindfulness practices. Improving your ability to respect boundaries and thresholds is an absolute matter of the heart and mind. You must know yourself and take great care of yourself to better manage your emotions in conversation. In turn, you may increase your empathy and compassion for the well-being of others. Healthy dialogue and threatening conversation activate different areas of the brain and need different self-care techniques. Know what makes you tick. Know what makes you feel safe or threatened. Know what upsets you and what calms you. Know what you can and cannot handle. And know when to say when.

CHAPTER 5

Ask #3
Practice No Judgment

Ask #3, which requests one to practice no judgment as a listener, is vital for the achievement of safer spaces. For better or worse, no one knows you like you do. Even those closest to you might be surprised to discover your innermost thoughts and feelings. The truth is people know the version of you with whom you have permitted them to have exposure or connection. And even then you do not have power over how you are perceived and received. At every turn in human engagement, people carry values, opinions, and beliefs about anything and everything imaginable. Radical folks with enough discipline, wisdom, and maturity may reach a level of self-awareness and confidence to be unaffected by the opinions of others. In those rare instances, Ask #3 doesn't matter as much. For supernaturally confident people, judgment has little impact on their ability to feel safe, brave, or courageous in spaces with other humans. For the vast majority, though, people care what others think of them. In the absence of knowing what others think and without power to change minds, gain favor, or even successfully people please, humans often default to blocking their deepest and truest authenticity to prevent their purest selves from being the subject of judgment. Ask #3 beseeches us to soften our imposed values, opinions, and biases about others and give folks the opportunity to be genuine without the infliction of judgment.

Red Light: What to Stop, Look, and Listen For

Take a moment to reflect on people, places, things, and ideas that evoke fear, discomfort, dislike, or disdain inside of you. Do you know the origin stories of your opinions, values, biases, and judgments? Scholar and author Trabian Shorters discusses stigma and threat when teaching on his paradigm about asset-framing (as opposed to deficit model thinking), especially as it relates to neurological and emotional impulses. Dr. Shorters shares that when we see or experience something we perceive as a threat, our first impulse is to avoid it. If we cannot avoid it, our next impulse is to try to control it. If we cannot avoid or control that which makes us feel threatened, our impulse is to kill the threat. Adding to Dr. Shorters's framework, we fear what we don't understand. Therefore, we try to control what we don't understand. And what we can't control, we kill. Judgment is part of this evolution of thought. Judgment, particularly preconceived judgment of others, kills our ability to get to truly see, know, understand, and build relationships with others. This lack of understanding can lead to danger, threat, and harm. It allows for objective viewpoints, personal value systems, and deeply engrained opinions to pose as the truth. When linked to characteristics that society has classified as better than or worse than, judgment can result in far more detrimental things like bias and bigotry. Most folks would not describe themselves as biased, prejudiced, or bigoted. However, judgment of others can lead to unwelcome behavior, rejection, or, worse, harm. Disenfranchisement and danger are possible unintended outcomes whenever we ascribe our own perception of value and worth on something or someone else. In order to not judge (or even to judge less), as Ask #3 requests of us, it might help to further interrogate our judgments' root causes.

Where did these judgments come from? Imagine our brain is a file cabinet with seemingly infinite capacity that has catalogued every piece of information ever received by categories including but not limited to descriptions, names, origin stories, and values. We didn't immediately know how to feel about all the people, places, things, and ideas to which we have been introduced. Much of that information was given to us by the most influential people in our lives. Parents or guardians told us what was dangerous. We were guided in educational systems by teachers, administrators, and support staff on what was worth learning and what was not. Peers taught us in word and deed about the hierarchy of social status. Jobs trained us on what was profitable to focus on (and why). And heaven knows the media perfected the imperfect science of teaching us what was beautiful, entertaining, valuable, dangerous, and desirous, especially for the purposes of emulation. By the time we gain more lived experiences and increase our exposure to conflicting information in our folders, the originally implanted idea has long become what some might refer to as an implicit or unconscious bias. This is one of many possible origin stories on where judgment comes from, which is why it takes a great deal of bravery and courage to unlearn and relearn what we think we know about ourselves and others.

Are my beliefs factual and true? If we desire to create safer, braver, and more courageous spaces, arguably one of the most important questions we must ask ourselves is, "Can I prove that my opinions about people, places, things, and ideas *are empirically true?*" Consider that everything we learn, including information fed to our youngest and most impressionable minds, we have implicitly coded as absolute truth. What happens, though, if the first piece of information about a person, place, thing, or idea is not true? How would a child know their information foundation was faulty? We do not immediately teach young minds to think critically. Would a child know the difference between the truth and their guardian's personal value system? Moreover, do we give children the right to disagree, correct, or push back against adults if and when they discover or believe a trusted adult's information is incorrect or biased? When we are young, we are in precarious positions with the given expectations to trust those who deposit the first items into the folders of our file cabinets. We are cautioned to assume an old or familiar notion is a correct notion.

Am I committed to my unconscious biases? The practice of no judgment asks us to be modest, lowering ourselves in importance and dominance so that we create space for and value others. At times, we may desire to change our thinking, but we struggle to do so. In other moments or instances, we simply don't want to let go of the old judgment. Even in the face of rigorous data, some remain in denial if the facts don't align with their fiction or feelings. Moreover, the older, stronger, or deeper a judgment is, the harder it may be to interrupt or fracture it. Change is hard. Even if it isn't difficult, sometimes we just don't want to change. Judgment is easy and often automatic; unlearning and relearning is much harder. Be mindful of moments when implicit bias or judgment is so deeply imbedded, it seems impossible to think differently. This may be a sign that your opinions are more than just judgments; they may be core beliefs.

Yellow Light: Proceed to Practice with Caution

Is it time to change your mind? Even in nature, new seasons call for a cleaning out of the old to create space for the new. We have control over noticing, interrupting, and ending misinformation and disinformation. Practicing the third of the Nine Asks has the power to enhance our minds while it softens our hearts. No longer locked in the cycle of fear, misunderstanding, control, and destruction, letting go of judgment gives us permission to be brave and courageous. We have consent to be curious. We have freedom to flow. We have external and internal approval to create new ideas and relationships. Suspending judgment allows something new and different to be true. When the unknown becomes known, it can be frightening or exhilarating. The choice to grow is yours.

Practice Example: "Wise Counsel for Moses and Malcolm"
Ms. Carmichael had been an advisor and counselor for twenty-two years when she inherited the case files for brothers Moses and

Malcolm, new transfers to Westhaven High School. The optics of their records fit the description of typical stereotypes for impoverished boys of color in public schools. Over two decades in education, Ms. Carmichael had lost many BIPOC male students to substance abuse, mass incarceration, mental illness, homelessness, and, tragically, death. Between her heavy caseload and lengthy career, she thought it best to spend her time on "squeaky wheel" students and scholars who were relentless in their pursuit of academic success. Moses and Malcolm were neither.

Malcolm was in constant trouble and tended to fill a room with his mouth and massive personality. His bravado evoked tension, both at home and away. Throughout high school, Malcolm had tremendous athletic ability but struggled academically and was often suspended for disciplinary issues. He had several acquaintances and a small circle of loyal but equally troublesome friends. His scrappiness gained him the reputation for being hot-tempered, arrogant, and unemotional. By senior year, he was labeled dangerous, threatening, and a menace. Moses, on the other hand, three years Malcolm's junior, was private, shy, and introverted. He shrank in stature, voice, and visibility as a survival and coping strategy. Desperate to avoid repercussions exacerbated by his older brother's notoriety, the little brother hid in plain sight. He ate alone. He seldom spoke. He took on quirky personal hobbies as opposed to popular school activities, and he had close relationships with only one or two people outside of Malcolm. Most students and staff thought he was odd, if they noticed him at all. Moses was perceived to be quiet and weird, and subsequently, he was largely ignored and made fun of in school. He barely made it to graduation in one piece.

Malcolm and Moses met with Ms. Carmichael only a handful of times during their tenure at Westhaven. Both desired to attend college, but advising conversations didn't go far. Ms. Carmichael, a veteran in the field, had seen so many students like Malcolm and Moses before. Based on her experiences, the odds were high that Malcolm would end up dead or in jail and Moses would likely fade away into a mundane, average, and uneventful life. Years later, the brothers attended a high school reunion. Returning alumni and staff—Ms. Carmichael included—were shocked to discover that Malcolm became an elected official after graduate school. And Moses, the wallflower brother, had amassed considerable financial status and success as the founder of a logistics company. Family, friends, and various adults judged and sentenced the brothers to failure and mediocrity before their eighteenth birthdays. Had it not been for Malcolm's and Moses's self-knowledge and determination, they could have easily become the stigmatized statistics imposed on them. Ms. Carmichael was in a position of authority and power over their lives. But instead of helping, she perpetuated harm by disregarding their worth. She judged and saw bad seeds; however, had she noticed her (pre)judgment of them and corrected her biased thoughts, she would have discovered they were diamonds in the rough.

Heavy is the head that wears the crown. Those in positions of power carry great responsibility regarding Ask #3. While judgment may seem like an innocent idiosyncrasy of human existence, the judgments of those in charge can wield a great deal of influence and impact. How far can the ripple effect of judgment go? Can judgment impact where one lives, learns, worships, or works? Yes, judgment in its most extreme form threatens to debilitate one's very quality of life. Look no further than members of the global majority with the least amount of political power, such as Moses and Malcolm, whose rights have been impacted by judgment.

Judgment against people of color wearing braids or locs in school and workplaces has likewise caused harm. After innumerable bouts of discrimination against something as specific as hairstyles and hair texture, The CROWN Act ("CROWN" being an acronym for Create a Respectful and Open World for Natural Hair) was cofounded by Dove and the CROWN Coalition with partners including the National Urban League, Color of Change, and the Western Center on Law and Poverty in 2019. It is state-based law that aims to put an end to race-based hair discrimination, which disproportionately affects Black people. As of September 2024, twenty-seven states (including the District of Columbia) have passed CROWN laws, but it is still legal in nearly half of the United States to discriminate in academic and professional spaces based on hair and hair texture.

Leaders may forget, overlook, not consider, or have never experienced the threat to safety when being judged, particularly by folks who have power over them. And what happens to one's pursuit of safety when there's judgment at every turn? This is the reality of people who are judged for being too much in one space and not enough somewhere else. Too feminine for men but not feminine enough according to other women. Too Asian for whites but not Asian enough for elder Asians. Too comfortable to be poor but too broke to be rich. Biases, especially when experienced within and outside of one's reference groups, can inform the way one sees oneself and can lead to the following unhealthy coping strategies:

Self-fulfilling prophecy. Sometimes our expectations of a person, place, thing, or idea can be so strong that they influence and change behaviors, and eventually our expectation of someone else becomes their reality. For example, if we believe a certain person is angry and if we always judge and treat them as if they are angry, they may eventually become angry with us. However, it is important to note that anger was not the person's original demeanor or personality attribute. Judgment and negative treatment of them led to anger. Our thoughts and behaviors are powerful, and all energy can become a contagion.

Cultural code-switching. This behavioral phenomenon involves modifying—or even hiding—unique expressions, behaviors, choices, and general portrayal of one's authentic self to better blend or fit in with the dominant culture. Performative behaviors, such as disguising an accent, avoiding ethnic food in public, straightening or covering curly hair, or participating in undesirable activities to be accepted by the group might occur when it felt easier or safer to avoid judgment by not being yourself.

Invisibility. Some avoid judgment by flying under the radar and seeking invisibility. By making oneself unnoticeable and undetectable, it seems possible to prevent or minimize judgment from others. Like Moses, invisible folks do not ruffle feathers. They do not speak up. They do not disagree or dissent. They do not emote feelings. They may even opt to make choices in a fashion or self-expression that mute, block, repel, or redirect any attention from themselves. The danger is that invisibility may imply unimportance and insignificance.

How do we begin the process of divesting in behaviors that result in dysregulating and self-minimizing coping strategies? How do we convince folks that they're worthy of judgment-free acceptance? In our safest states, humans desire to have their humanity honored by being seen, heard, and appreciated. Our work seeks to disrupt danger with safety. Practitioners of the Nine Asks see the value in honoring and fighting for the safety and humanity of others, even if (and when) we don't get the practice right every time. Fret not; frustration when trying a new thing is an inevitability. This is a good time to remember that grace abounds in the practice of Ask #2 as well as all the other Asks. Consider these tips to get through the practice of Ask #3 with less judgment and more grace and compassion:

Slow down. Faster is not always better, especially when it comes to being careful in the treatment of others and thoughtful in the reframing of our minds and memories. According to psychotherapist Dr. Lou Cozolino, humans process conscious thoughts in about five hundred to six hundred milliseconds. Unconscious or implicit thoughts, especially those rooted in fear, move about ten times faster. Be gentle with yourself. Slow down and pace yourself.

Relate through your story. Pushing back against the temptation to judge when listening to others requires us to accept that a person's intimate lived experience is truer than the compromised information in our brain files. Credible storytellers are to be trusted and believed, not their stigmas and stereotypes. People should not be reduced to nightly news or newspaper headlines and isolated experiences we have had with someone who shared a singular identity lens they possess.

Separate numbers from narratives. Know the difference as well as the relationship between statistics and stories. Any figure or piece of data can be engineered to benefit the storyteller. Reflect on the narrative in accompaniment with the number. For example, data on people experiencing housing insecurity may be factual. However, engaging in a meaningful conversation with an unhoused person might dispel stigma and stereotypes and minimize judgment.

Heal in affinity spaces. If you have been the recipient of unfair judgment, especially in the company of folks who are very different from you, seek some time at home or with people who know you most and love you best. There is nothing wrong with pausing to find comfort in people who share a meaningful identity lens with you and are unlikely to judge you. It's important to remember how that feels so that you can pay the feeling forward.

Be curious instead of critical. When we encounter a person whose appearance or behavior looks and feels different from what we perceive to be familiar or safe, we often label said individual as abnormal or displaying behavior that is wrong. "What happened?" is much more inviting for conversation than, "What's wrong with you?" A trauma-informed, more humane, and healing-centered framework is to presume folks can be different from you without being defective. Replacing judgment with healthy curiosity can transform and soften social interaction.

Green Light: Go Forth and Be Great

Practicing no judgment is a heavy but doable lift requiring transformation in both the head and the heart. Practitioners of this Ask must be brave enough to examine their thinking, have a willingness to learn something new, and perhaps have the gumption to spread the good news of no judgment when and wherever possible. When we change our minds about others, we have the chance to change our actions and our impact on the lives of others, too. Take a moment and acknowledge some of the ways, such as those listed below, in which you build equity by valuing fellow humans when you make spaces safer through nonjudgment:

Staying uncomfortable. There may be a little discomfort when catching and correcting judgmental thoughts as we improve our practice of Ask #3. However, we grow when we are uncomfortable, especially through the art of engaging in meaningful dialogue. The Art of Hosting is a school of thought that offers approaches to creating deeper conversations.

Within this paradigm, the natural energy of the world is explained as the chaordic path. This word, *chaordic*, has been credited to the founder of Visa, Dee Hock. Illustrated with a Venn diagram, the chaordic path asserts that human systems range in energy flow from chaos to order. The extreme of chaos is collapse. When too much chaos distracts us, we do not grow. The extreme of order is control. When too much order bores us, we do not grow. But right in the middle of the Venn diagram where the chaos bubble intersects with the order bubble, there is a sweet spot called the chaordic path. In moments of tender space, we are given the opportunity to learn, create, and grow. There's a comfort in our passive permission of implicit bias and judgment. It's time to get uncomfortable.

Forming new neuropathways. Neuroscientists have identified an ability our brains have called neuroplasticity. This fancy word means our brains can continually grow and adapt. As it turns out, we are not hardwired. We are not trapped in old, erroneous, judgmental mindsets and behaviors. Our brains are malleable and can rewire themselves to function differently than before. We can heal from experiences that harmed us, and we can change stinkin' thinkin' that has harmed others. When we rewrite the truths about others based on how they show and tell their stories to us, we scientifically and miraculously receive the gift of a renewed mind.

Accepting the new you. Much of this chapter addresses external judgment from one person to another. An added element is the consideration of self-judgment. As your mind opens, you may become internally critical of yourself and judge your old ways of biased thinking and being. However, your continuous improvement is evidence that you're doing the courageous work of checking yourself and interrupting your implicit bias. We can be liberated from hate. We can create spaces and places where acceptance rather than assimilation and belongingness, not bigotry of others, can abide.

Ask #3's practice of no judgment is a solid gesture for extending goodwill to others. For those who lean into its application and truly improve their efforts to reduce judgment, Ask #3 is a great investment in oneself as well. It's a win-win way to co-construct containers of safety. Remain open to the possibility that new information can come from anyone and anywhere. Be amenable to the idea that anyone of any background and identity at any given time can be the teacher that a moment and a receptive mind needs. The *Tao Te Ching* is credited with the quote, "When the student is ready, the teacher will appear. When the student is really ready, the teacher will disappear." Stay present and don't miss your moment to grow.

CHAPTER 6

Ask #4
Honor Confidentiality

Ask #4, to honor confidentiality, recognizes our roles as storytellers and story recipients. It challenges us to contemplate what ownership of narratives really means. This Ask recognizes the narrator as the only authority with power, permission, and appointed control over their story. In the ultimate pursuit of safer and braver spaces, confidentiality asserts that unless one has given another communicated permission, a person's story—particularly unauthorized—should never be told by someone else. The storyteller is and will always be the originator, creator, and owner of the intellectual property that is their story, and they offer themselves, through the gift of their story, to the receiver. In exchange, the storyteller seeks for the gift to be kept, treasured, and well taken care of. Honoring confidentiality assumes trust, and trusting people is so hard. Here are some things that threaten trust on the road to practicing confidentiality:

No guarantees. Trust is a phenomenally difficult virtue to experience and exchange with another human being. It is sometimes described as assured reliance. Strength is often referenced as a virtue one needs to have trust and to be trustworthy. Things go awry when folks cannot be guaranteed that others have enough discipline to be entrusted to hold the gift of their story and not play show-and-tell with it.

History of harm. Distressing past experiences make trust a bit more complex and complicated to earn. Remember, our brains are designed to protect and take care of us. A brain that has survived hurt and harm will position itself as chief of security detail and scan every environment—including the people in it—for surveillance of new threats, especially those that remind it of a previous source of danger. Trusting and confiding in others may feel dangerous for some, and for a trauma survivor, danger is to be averted at all costs.

Violation of translation. Telephone is a game played by many youths during recess. It involves whispering a statement to someone, who then repeats the statement as accurately as they can to the next person in line, and so on through a line of message recipients. Most times, the final recipient of the statement shares aloud what they believe they have been told, and usually the message shared is a far cry from that which was expressed by the original speaker. The risk of a listener "playing telephone" with someone's story by passing it through multiple hearers is losing the truth in translation.

Privacy versus secrecy. There is a difference between private information and a secret. Semantics, definitions, and our personal experiences support this assertion. Privacy is described as consensual, nonthreatening, and a conscious decision to confide. Secrecy, on the other hand, alludes to disingenuous intent. New practitioners of Ask #4 would likely prefer to explore trust by being treated as if their stories are confidential and courageous as opposed to dirty little secrets.

Red Light: What to Stop, Look, and Listen For

Ask #4 is about information ownership and possession. Those who ask for the honoring of confidentiality are imploring for intact power and control over their stories. A storyteller may have no issue with sharing their story with others; the caveat is they want to have the choice on whether to share their story or not. When we lose choice regarding if or how the story is told, the safety, bravery, and courage in a space is broken. Leaks and breaches like those listed below are hazards to watch out for when guarding our story gifts:

The "open-book" leak. Most of us have made the acquaintance of a person who describes themselves as an open book. These folks are not bound to censorship in any way and feel complete freedom in sharing every salacious detail of their stories to whoever is an interested listener. For them, their narrative details exist in a free market for open consumption. The challenge is if you are part of any of their stories, it is a safe bet that your information has been freely sacrificed as well. A person who lacks discretion or boundaries regarding their own business is not likely to show discretion or boundaries for yours.

The "groupthink" leak. Nigerian writer Chimamanda Ngozi Adichie gained great acclaim with her TED Talk "The Danger of a Single Story."[2] In it, she posits that when we compress individual identities into broad brush-stroked categories, we are at risk of imposing assumptions and conclusions on folks without ever knowing who they really are. There is no monolith in categorical identity. There is no such thing as one Black story. One immigrant story. One poverty story. A person who believes your story is the same as theirs because you share a singular identity marker (this includes family or a friendship circle) will have no internal conflict with telling your story to others, especially within your shared affinity group.

The "keepin' it real" leak. There are some who will lead you to believe that they value transparency and honesty and that it comes in the form of telling other folks' business as well as their own. "I didn't think I was telling your business; I was just trying to be honest and transparent." Do not let Ask #1, Be as Honest and Vulnerable as Possible, be the excuse for a lack of decorum and a violation of Ask #4, Honor Confidentiality.

Special note: There are some extenuating circumstances when confidentiality can create more danger than safety. When someone is being harmed in secrecy, it demands an automatic information leak for someone's urgent safety, health, and wellness. Unlike leaks, mandated reporting is designed as an emergency measure to protect the storyteller and others from abuse or neglect.

Yellow Light: Proceed to Practice with Caution

As the owners of our narratives, we are its sole credible witness. Should someone else attempt to tell our stories for us, there is a risk of addition or omission that invalidates the narrative. If information is added to the story that is not true, the narrative no longer belongs to its owner. If information is omitted or deleted from the story, it equally becomes an untrue account of one's voice. The only way to honor the clarity, authenticity, and totality of a story is for its creator, originator, and owner to be the lone teller of the tale. Envision that each time you share your story with someone, what you are doing is giving them the gift of you. It would be a breach of trust as well as a form of dishonor for said person to give your precious gift to another person. That is essentially what happens when we tell other people's stories *for* them and without their permission to do so.

Practice Example: "The Story of Solomon's Lion"
It could be argued that we enter and exit this realm of life with three things: our bodies, our beingness, and our word. When our words are taken away from us, it diminishes our control over how we shape and experience our realities. It impacts our choices with respect to if and how we create our legacies. This disempowerment or removal of access to power has existed in all lands and throughout the course of time and history. An embodiment of this point—and why it matters—can be explicitly illustrated in the infamous story of the legendary folk song "The Lion Sleeps Tonight."

One's age, nationality, and preferred music genre impacts how your introduction to this song came to be. If you are a fan of the legendary Disney film and now Broadway musical *The Lion King*, the song is a familiar tune playfully sung by lovable characters Timon and Pumbaa from the animated film and stage production. *The Lion King* film was released in 1994. However, since 1951, "The Lion Sleeps Tonight" had been recorded and released by a minimum of twelve different music acts, including but not limited to the Weavers, Jimmy Dorsey, Yma Sumac, Noro Morales, the Kingston Trio, Miriam Makeba, The Tokens, Karl Denver, Henri Salvador, Tight Fit, R.E.M., and NSYNC.

Most people know and enjoy whimsically singing in falsetto to the chorus of the song, "The Lion Sleeps Tonight." However, few have ever heard of its original composer, Solomon Linda. His is the melancholy chronicle of a lost story due to disempowerment that extended for generations. Linda was an illiterate migrant laborer and South African vocalist who crooned the first-ever recording of the song. Legend has it, Linda recorded the song partially impromptu in his Zulu language in 1939, where it had notable success for nearly ten years in South Africa. Its original title was not "The Lion Sleeps Tonight" but rather "Mbube" (pronounced em-BOO-bay), which is Zulu for the word *lion*. In 1948, however, visitors from other continents who were enthusiasts of folk music heard Linda's song, imported a recording back to the United States, adapted some of the vocal arrangements, wrote new, English lyrics (as they did not understand or speak Zulu), and achieved great success. "Mbube" was translated to "Wimoweh" (an incorrect pronunciation of the word "Uyimbube," which means "you are a lion") and then to "The Lion Sleeps Tonight." The authenticity of the song was irreparably distorted and diminished, and when US music producers claimed publishing rights on "The Lion Sleeps Tonight" and copyrighted it for legal ownership, Solomon Linda's first-person narrative composition was erased. After decades of capitalism-infused legal and political battles over its intellectual property, Linda finally received authorship credit for the song. Sadly, by the time Solomon Linda was recognized as the original composer of what became "The Lion Sleeps Tonight," he had transitioned into death (still in poverty), and his family had inherited small amounts of money but large volumes of generational trauma directly and indirectly related to years of struggle and court battles.

There is power in being clearly and explicitly identified as the creator and only authorized communicator of one's story. Solomon Linda lost power and control over his art and effectively his story. His is a cautionary tale of what is possible when Ask #4, Honor Confidentiality, is violated repeatedly, both personally and professionally. In the absence of "ultimate" power (e.g., white, straight, male, educated, Christian, English-speaking identity), choice in how our narratives are created and shared is iteratively reduced. Power, control, bias, and prejudice are invariably embedded in all human systems, even structures intended to be benevolent. The fewer choices folks have, the less power and control they have over what happens to their stories and, in extreme cases, if they are perceived to have a story at all. Without respect for the application of confidentiality, people risk losing ownership of the proverbial masters to their own voices.

"Man makes plans; God laughs." Even when we earnestly plan to approach engagement with good intentions, things can go awry in the execution. The need for confidentiality through the application of Ask #4 emerges when stories go a little deeper, when we ask for a little more information, or when context requires us to go further and make it a little more personal. When we are better practitioners of Ask #4, power is restored in each sentient being to determine when, how, and how much of their stories are told. Privilege or unearned access should not be a determining factor in who gets to own, keep, and share their stories. Our stories are our birthright. Everyone should have the power to choose how, when, where, and with whom they enact the power of voice. Consider these speed bumps when traversing the path of practicing Ask #4 to honor confidentiality:

Exposing vulnerable populations. A critical component in all the Nine Asks and most especially regarding Ask #4 is the consideration of power differential. When power and control are uneven and inequitable between the storyteller and the story recipient, people to be taken advantage of and trust can be mismanaged. In the absence of consciousness and culturally competent behavior, it is easier to slip up, share other folks' stories without context, consent, or compassion, and ultimately violate Ask #4. Worse, in spaces where there is a perversion of power and control over vulnerable populations, persons in positions of perceived power may incorrectly believe they have the authority to violate confidentiality. A child, especially among adults, could be considered a member of a vulnerable population. A woman might be considered a vulnerable population member when sharing her story with a man. A person of color may possibly be a vulnerable population member when their sacred stories are sacrificed in predominantly white spaces.

Fumbling in informal spaces. There are some settings where it is unspoken and understood that the sharing of personal information is frowned on. One would be less likely to share explicit personal matters about themselves or others with elected officials or royalty. One might even be less inclined to share personal information with an elder as opposed to a peer. However, in an informal setting, there tends to be a much more liberal announcement of personal business. Information sharing is less constrained. Informal spaces are not and should never be guaranteed indicators that it is permissible to violate the confidentiality required by Ask #4. Whether the audience is royalty, elected officials, people of wealth, or common, salt-of-the-earth good folks, a person's story is still their own. Without uncontested ownership of our personal narratives and our voices in any and every environment, few spaces will be truly safe.

And after the sharing is complete . . .

Think before you teach. When someone shares information with you as a credible storyteller of their personal experience, you may feel impacted by the information. Perhaps it blossoms into a reflective moment or shift in consciousness for you. Like the folk music enthusiasts who first were mesmerized by Linda's song, you may want to share this epiphany with others. Be careful not to reteach and re-share their story as if it is your own. Remember, their story does not belong to you. The storyteller is the author. You are a benefactor of their story. Your only rightful possession in this exchange is enlightenment (which you can share freely if desired).

Request permission to share. One of the foundational ways to honor the practice of Ask #4 is to simply gain the permission of the storyteller. Perhaps context is necessary and helpful for greater impact in expanding the reach, power, and students of a story. To do so, you may desire to share more than Cliffs-Notes; you may wish to share someone's whole story. In the matter of full story retelling, simply ask the person, "May I share your story with others?" You might be surprised that a narrator may be open and willing to be transparent and public regarding the gift of their story broadcasted to a larger audience. Should the original author grant permission for you to be authorized to regift, make sure to give the story proper context. Make sure to give them credit. That way, you can still fully and completely honor Ask #4.

Dignify an ask for anonymity. While we should always default to give credit where credit is due, some people feel safer influencing and impacting others through powerful words and deeds with the caveat of anonymity. Consider, for example, the importance of anonymity for self-help gurus whose content features former clients or for justice-involved individuals who seek advocacy but not the negative attention that comes with the bias of incarceration. We can play a positive role in protecting the identities of storytellers when safety looks like confidentiality through anonymity. Seek the wise counsel of the storyteller to gauge their desired level of privacy; then honor it.

Reciprocate when ready. There is an African proverb that says, "Many hands make the load light." Sharing is risky, personal, and uncomfortable. We can make the heaviness easier by completing the feedback loop through the sharing of our own story. Reciprocity is a key practice in the creation of safer, braver spaces. It is much harder to violate an Ask when we are extending the same request to someone else. The stakes are higher for me to be a good steward in the creation of safer spaces when my safety is incumbent on your better implementation of the Nine Asks. We both have something to gain, and we both have something to lose if we believe that safer spaces are developed through co-creation, co-design, and co-sustained practice.

Green Light: Go Forth and Be Great

In addition to trust, Ask #4, Honor Confidentiality, demonstrates a commitment to the virtues of respect and belongingness to take the practice to the next level. When we find a groove of not just an adequate amount of respect but a preferred and agreed on amount of respect for another human being, spaces become safer. When we are in alignment regarding a shared cadence of sustained belongingness that flows in a seamless and complementary way, we tap into a level of bravery unparalleled and we neutralize threat in human spaces. And as discussed throughout this chapter, when we are successful in establishing and, more importantly, *earning* sincere and believable trust from our fellow beings in human systems, spaces become more courageous than we can ever imagine. At the apex of the combined virtuous experiences we have sewn through confidentiality, we hope to reap these three lovely fruits of Ask #4:

The fruit of integrity. Even when we are greatly impacted . . . even when the story is phenomenal . . . even when we know others could benefit from the story of someone else's lived experience, it is the right thing to do to allow the storyteller to own their story and to decide if, when, and how it should be shared. There is a moral imperative at play with the practice of confidentiality, and it implores us to honor a person's wishes over our urge for automatic information dissemination. Even when the story is compelling or salacious, integrity ultimately encourages us to do the right thing and do right by the voice and narrative of those who have confided in us.

The fruit of mutuality. There are no shortcuts to attaining some of our most treasured and desired virtues. You must give love to receive love. You must practice patience to have patience.

You must demonstrate vulnerability to receive its benefits. Confidentiality, too, must be extended to demonstrate we are worthy recipients to receive it when it's our turn to share. The gift of mutuality is evidence of a braver and more courageous ecosystem and is possible only through the sustained, collective labor of love.

The fruit of fellowship. Through the experience of belongingness, there may be no greater feeling than having a confidante or a person in whom we can share closeness and transparency on private matters. Human beings spend a lifetime attempting to balance public experiences with private thoughts while staying sane. We have emotions and feelings that we sometimes struggle to navigate. Having a confidante to lean on can make the most difficult of times manageable and can feed are our deepest human desires to connect and belong.

Imagine being trusted as a soft place to land for someone overflowing with feelings of joy, sorrow, anger, or calm. Then envision yourself expanding your network of folks to whom you can hand over your tender emotions and experiences. When we get Ask #4 right and can have a consistent and believable practice of honorable confidentiality, it allows others to (co)regulate and release without worrying about what will happen to the integrity of their narratives. When we can share effortlessly and feel earnestly comforted by the care someone gives to the delicacy of our stories, we bear witness to the flowering fruit of our seed of trust. Through continual nurturing, that seed can grow, and we can harvest trust in others as well. Felt safety, bravery, and courage is rare air. Breathe it in. Enjoy the sweetness of Ask #4.

CHAPTER 7

Ask #5
Come Back to Me

Have you ever found yourself either rushed or ignored when in conversation with someone else? Perhaps you desired to share, but you just needed a little more time to get your thoughts and ideas together. Ask #5, Come Back to Me, is designed to provide time and space when we are not ready or when we don't yet feel safe enough to participate. Conditions of this Ask involve one-on-one situations and group settings. A physical space might be constructed with every option available to ensure safety, including but not limited to locked doors, closed windows, and familiar people nearby. We might even trust the person with whom we share a space in that we do not believe the person intends to inflict harm on us. However, nothing compares to internal felt safety. When we don't feel safe on the inside, there will never be enough features to convince us we're safe on the outside. Again our heads can lie, and our hearts can lie. But our bodies never lie. Ask #5 is an alert in human spaces that we need a moment to pause and gain clarity in our thoughts and feelings before engaging. It's a flashing light indicating that a safety need is not yet met in the conversation dynamics, and we are asking for more time to feel and implicitly believe we are safe to engage.

The application of Ask #5, Come Back to Me, in human engagement is unique because it can be impacted by the temperaments and personalities of the folks in the space. Information processing approach (or the way we think), communication styles, and human energy currents influence one another. Often, loquacious, loud, or high energy is the behavior that prompts those with shy, quiet, and lower energy to ask folks to come back to them as opposed to shutting down and disengaging in a shared space. According to a study done by the Myers-Briggs Type Indicator organization, nearly 60 percent of the world prefers extroversion. This number is likely inflated due to societal messaging that elevates more gregarious personalities. More specifically, people in positions of leadership often feel pressure to have a more extroverted communication style. In reality, more folks experience comfort and safety in introversion than extroversion. Below are two key elements that will thread through this chapter to aid us in understanding how the ups and downs of Ask #5 show up in our lives:

1. *Information processing and communication style.* How we take in and think through information is a component of our communication patterns. Our preferred approaches and methodologies for disseminating information to others are also shaped by our interactions. When you need to work through big feelings, is it better for you to be alone or with others? Do you prefer silence or sound in your professional and spiritual spaces? Do you produce your best work on solo projects or in teams? Do you cut to the chase, or are you prone to telling long stories? Depending on your orientation, you will either feel ease or face blind spots when someone asks you to come back to them.

2. *Energy flow.* Vibrational energy is everywhere, and in shared spaces, it is contagious. We are both senders and receivers of this energy. We can be both elevated or depleted by this energy. The energy can be heavy or light or anywhere in between. There is fluidity in the energy that exists between humans, and one of the most common currents for this energy is communication.

Consider your capacity to come back to someone or to circle around, re-invite and reengage a person who is hesitant to jump in and connect with others. This chapter will examine specific temperaments of introversion, extroversion, ambiversion, and empathy (see chart on the following page). It's important to know which temperament you are to better understand how you show up in spaces, how others may perceive you, and what you need to do to make others feel safer when in community together.

Ask #5's request that we remember to re-invite the voices of those who need time to reflect before sharing is a difficult ask for a person who naturally feels comfortable in speaking with immediacy. The three points listed below will more specifically identify the difficulty in getting this Ask right for ourselves and others. Our communication styles and temperaments speak loudly. As soon as we do—or do not—open our mouths, others likely lock in an expectation of how it will feel to engage others in conversation. Yes, bias is difficult to catch, block, and correct in human interaction. While there may be elements of truth in stigmas and stereotypes, limiting individuals to identify only within the constraints of perceptions of others is a recipe for disaster, often taking the shape of bias and bigotry. Know who you are and how your blind spots show up. When we know better, we can do better.

Red Light: What to Stop, Look, and Listen For

Practice Example: "Annie Needs a Minute"
Terri and Annie were opposite personalities who were drawn to each other and became fast friends. Over the years, the best friends were inseparable and thrived from the diversity of their differing temperaments and communication styles. While both had strengths in empathy, Annie was mild mannered and had an introverted, quiet nature. She preferred solo hobbies and to stay out of the limelight. Though extraordinarily talented, she gravitated toward low-key people and activities and secure, predictable employment where she could excel in solitude. Meanwhile, Terri was a wildflower. She was highly social, had lots of acquaintances, and often gravitated toward environments and experiences that were highly stimulating.

The Four Temperaments		
Introversion	Communication Style and Information Processing	• Sees more than others but says less. • Thinks before speaking. • Processes information internally. • Prefers additional time to receive and review information. • Doesn't share thoughts with others until they are complete and, often, unless asked to share externally. • Defaults to thorough thinking for clarity and understanding.
	Energy Flow	• Experiences more energy alone and less energy in the company of others. • Social activity, even if enjoyable, depletes energy.
Extroversion	Communication Style and Information Processing	• Speaks before or while thinking; thinks out loud, even if thought is not fully formed. • Doesn't need content or context to contribute to conversation. • Processes information externally. • Makes meaning as they speak. • Defaults to external communication for clarity and understanding.
	Energy Flow	• Experiences more energy in the company of others and less energy alone. • Social activity, whether with family and friends or strangers, is exhilarating and energy-giving. • In solitude, feels less stimulated and perhaps even fatigued.

Ambiversion	Communication Style and Information Processing	• Experiences hybrid communication style with both introversion and extroversion tendencies. • Blends internal and external processing patterns and preferences. • Adapts behavior to talk when less comfortable doing so and to refrain from speaking when talking is preferred. • Prefers gathering information prior to sharing thoughts and ideas but conditioned to ideate orally when asked.
	Energy Flow	• Feels energized by specific people or specific human interaction, then experiences relief and relaxation when social interaction is complete. • Energy experience and engagement is conditional with fluctuation and flow dependent on many different variables.
Empathy	Communication Style and Information Processing	• Tends to be highly perceptive of and sensitive to others' feelings and emotions. • The emotions of others impact the effectiveness of information processing.
	Energy Flow	• Experiences heightened intuitive receptivity. • Positive and negative energy of human spaces felt strongly with an ability to feel one's own bodily and spiritual energy. • Energy experience is similar to ambiversion with self-care needs most like introversion.

It was common for Terri to boldly take center stage, receive spotlight attention, and garner accolades for her humanitarian efforts in the community. Terri was a risk-taker at work, too, eventually leaving her secure career for social entrepreneurship.

Desiring to dream big with her best friend, Terri pushed, nudged, and pleaded for Annie to join her latest venture as a business partner after many failed attempts at ideas in the past. Annie was extremely hesitant but gave in to Terri's insistence with an uncertain yes. Terri, lost in her own excitement, missed the signs and signals of Annie's discomfort. She pressed her foot on the gas and began moving the start-up business forward at the speed of light. Annie feared her acquiescence to Terri's request to be a business partner might have been a bad decision with negative consequences ahead; she was right. Terri flooded Annie with texts, emails, and calls about the business. She pressured Annie to give feedback and to make major decisions with little time or information. The slower Annie's response was, the more frequently Terri made moves without her. Not only that, but Terri's pace gave no time for Annie to think, decompress, or regulate herself when she felt overwhelmed.

Annie grew to dread communication from Terri and found herself avoiding contact. After months of irregular engagement, Terri confronted her best friend and business partner with frustration about Annie's lack of involvement and leadership. Though usually quiet and reserved, Annie responded with a resignation from the business and a request that they take a moment to create some space in their friendship as well. Terri was shocked and devastated. Days of silence turned to weeks and then months. When the friends finally reconciled, Annie started by telling Terri she needed a minute. Annie used space and reflection to set new boundaries for her friendship with Terri, which included her commitment to herself that she would never again mix business with pleasure. The greatest lesson, however, was Terri's. She learned the hard way that her temperament and communication style had taken up too much room and created a threatening space for someone she deeply loved. Not coming back to Annie when she was ready nearly cost Terri a friendship.

Mandatory human interaction never produces connection. We should never force engagement if folks are not ready. When discomfort of any kind is felt, our bodies, minds, and spirits attempt to take care of us. Sometimes these implicit responses and behaviors are helpful in navigating choppy communication waters; other times, they are not. When we feel unsafe, the likelihood increases that we will shut down, check out, and remove ourselves from engaging with others as Annie did with Terri. Terri missed a lot of Annie's warning signs that the space of their friendship was increasingly becoming unsafe. Examine the signs below for other things that might agitate an uncertain or unwilling participant in a shared space:

Noise. Unpleasant sound — expressed as speaking or not — is categorically a huge irritant. It is not as simple as being loud or silent. There are ways we can be more or less noisy. Sometimes it is by audible speech. Other times it is expressed in body language. Energy and emotional vibration can also be very loud or very quiet. The allergen of noise may show up in moments when the space gets quiet or stays quiet a little longer than desired. Annie's silence was a voice all by itself, and Terri initially missed the message. Something interesting could emerge by making room for a pregnant pause, such as the birth of a rich thought or idea following the silence. However, in the absence of good practice, our old "stinkin' thinkin'" kicks in. A moment of silence for an introvert can easily become a stalemate of silence with an absolute refusal to speak. Meanwhile, an extrovert may struggle to allow the silence its full moment, and they will speak too soon to fill the space with noise. Ambiverts may feel torn in how to respond when uncomfortable silence shows up and may default to either of the less desirable responses of the extrovert or introvert but for different reasons. All while the introvert, extrovert, and ambivert battle between silence and noise, the tension in the space can easily become too much for an empath and lead to them feeling overstimulated and either exploding or emotionally shutting down, due to an energy overload. There's so much more happening in a room than meets the eye.

Fear. In conversation and communication, it is of critical importance that we notice when fear shows up. More importantly, the next right thing may be to interrogate what are we afraid of. What do we fear will happen if we engage or continue to engage? What are we afraid will happen if we do not? Fear can turn an extrovert like Terri into a bully. Fear can turn an introvert like Annie into a wallflower. Fear can turn an ambivert into a chameleon. Fear can turn an empath into a dysregulated ball of nerves. Fear is a core emotion, and its experience is inevitable. Stay in constant maintenance of our relationship with self, which includes a foundational under-standing of how fear takes shape in our own consciences.

Why does this all matter? The ways we communicate, process information, and experience our bandwidth of energy informs our performance and approach in balancing all this in the midst of human engagement. When we are not aware of how we show up with regard to interaction and reflection temperament, we can be obtuse to the safety needs of others and inadvertently make spaces feel more threatening. When we come back to someone and reach back out to let them know their contributions are (still) welcome and desired, we get closer to reaching the right cadence of blended temperaments within the group. There's no rushing or dragging in the flow of engagement. There is time and room for everyone.

Yellow Light: Proceed to Practice with Caution

There are several ways the lofty practice of Ask #5, Come Back to Me, can fall flat. Sometimes the best of intentions can lead to unintended consequences. Blame it on being out of practice. Perhaps emotions and feelings got the best of us. Maybe we entered communication when we were already dysregulated and not in great mental, physical, or emotional condition. Watch out for the following mishaps in mindfulness when coming back to someone in conversation:

Fronting. Coming back to someone does not mean putting the spotlight of spectacle on them, especially in a group setting, and forcing them to speak on cue. Our job in practicing

Ask #5 is to offer a gracious opportunity to share, not to bully, someone into speaking.

Interrupting. While interrupting is not considered rude to everyone (especially if it is a normal phenomenon in your home, upbringing, or culture), it is rarely considered a positive or polite attribute in conversations that matter. Talking over a person may not always make a conversation dangerous, but it never makes a conversation safer.

Forgetting to re-invite contribution. Perhaps you were in conversation, noticed someone had not contributed, and invited them to share. That's awesome! However, if the practice of Ask #5 happens only once and never again, there is still no proof that conversation with you or in said space has the capacity or ability to be sustainably safe. Consistency is key for safety.

Running over comfortable time limits. Conversation can get unsafe rather quickly when someone dominates the space, the energy runs too high or too low, or the conversation extends longer or gets exponentially deeper than planned. Similarly, being curt, abrupt, and abbreviated—especially in the absence of noticing the feelings and emotions in human engagement—can be a recipe for destruction of a safer space. Curating the right amount of time, temperament, and flow matters and makes all the difference.

Mismanaging distractions. Voice is not the only element that can interrupt the flow of conversation. Babies crying, fire alarms, extreme room temperatures, malaise, and many other external factors can break concentration and force a reset of engagement. Disturbances of any kind can impede the positive flow of discourse, and worse, these kinds of interferences are typically out of our control. Practicing Ask #5, Come Back to Me, can get a little shaky if focus is broken. We must do our best to master redirection, regardless of the barriers.

Practice does not make perfect; it makes things permanent. Ask #5, Come Back to Me, is a request for continuous practice in the art of invitation. Personal improvement demands modification and evolution of natural communication behaviors. Without continuous practice, there will be irregularities and inconsistencies in how we honor ourselves and others in human engagement. Limited practice makes it difficult to see our barriers in communication, and we will be slower to notice the design and deeper needs of communicators around us. Make room for these suggested practices:

Unending invitations. Ask #5 is not a one-time offer. Practiced properly, one must be prepared to continually welcome temperaments less inclined to readily talk, such as introversion, back into conversation. The pattern of invitation communicates earnestness.

Variety in dialogue. There is not just one way to have a conversation. Additionally, the less traditional the format of conversation is, the higher the likelihood of reaping different results. Having and hosting conversations in different ways creates opportunities for different communication styles and temperaments to have moments to shine. Variety in Ask #5 conversation invitations might include deep questions, meaningful dialogue prompts, the Appreciative Inquiry model, fidget items for neurodivergent communicators, and artistic note-taking, such as graphic recording or visualization.

Controlled pacing and cadence. The faster the conversation cadence and the louder the conversation gets, the greater the possibility grows to lose the presence and participation of introverts, empaths, and ambiverts who are trying to balance their voice. When possible, slow down the communication speed to a manageable speed and watch your tone.

Ahead-of-time agendas. Though there can be an exciting energy in being sporadic and spontaneous, impromptu dialogue can feel chaotic. Some gifts and contributions emerge faster than others, and a quick idea is not necessarily the best one. Give folks talking points early, permitting everyone an equitable opportunity to ready themselves for contribution.

Strengths-based appreciations. The more thoughts, ideas, and emotions there are in a space, the more complex and complicated it becomes to sort it all out and negotiate the best outcomes. Let people know that regardless of the challenges that emerge in conversation, their gifts are needed, valued, and appreciated.

Note-taking. When in doubt, write it out. Consider making resources available for folks to write down their ideas, thoughts, and feelings as they pause and ponder. In addition to augmenting a solid reflection process, note-taking aids us in remembering important points, it distracts folks from interruption, and it can provide a regulating release of private feelings and emotions.

Temperament Tips for Ask #5

For extroverts, moments of extroversion cause you to speak and engage without thinking. Words flow like water, and that is not always a good thing. It may feel easier to fill up a space. Bravery for an extrovert may mean facing the discomfort of silence and bypassing the opportunity to speak and be heard. Here are three quick tips for the extrovert:

1. *Sit still.* If you typically get your energy from being around and engaged with others, try processing your energy differently. Notice the thoughts in your mind, the words in your throat, and the energy in your body. See what happens if you just sit with it all instead of immediately releasing your first words and thoughts.

2. *Let silence be a voice.* Silence can be an incredibly powerful communicator. It may feel like every statement needs a response, but a healthy hesitation or a pregnant pause may prove to be far more valuable in giving dialogue a moment to marinate.

3. *Hold that thought.* When allowing another person a moment to get their thoughts and ideas together and make a conscious decision of what they wish to share, practice retaining your thought or idea. Remain fully present to listen when others speak and share.

For introverted types, whether you entered the world in peace with privacy or you are designed to flex between a speaking and silent world, the introvert (and some ambiverts) will naturally gravitate to silence being golden. There may be ease and relief in taking it all in and reflecting on your own. Bravery for an introvert may mean facing the discomfort of speaking up and speaking out when silence would be so much simpler. Here are four quick tips for those who gravitate toward introversion:

1. *Speak up when it's time.* In human engagement, especially if words are moving fast and passionately, there may be a sweet spot that emerges and calls for a careful, thoughtful, conversational contribution. That is your moment to shine. Pay attention not only to what you notice and think but also to when it is time to share your words.

2. *Step into your gift and responsibility.* Contrary to popular belief, the person most comfortable speaking is not always the sole voice that needs to be heard in a space. As referenced earlier in this chapter, introversion is accompanied by some unique talents, gifts, and abilities that enrich people and ideas. Not only is the contribution of this gift needed, but also think of it as your responsibility as the host of the gift of introversion to be a good steward of your curated thoughts, words, and ideas. Sometimes it is important to share and engage for the greater good.

3. *Personally validate and value your role.* External affirmation isn't a given. Your value may sometimes be looked over in spaces, which, in turn, may make it easier to not speak up. This does not bother every introvert, but if it bothers you, know that your words have immense worth. Your kudos may not be extended publicly; however, the benefit of introversion in shared spaces is priceless.

4. *Open yourself up to support.* Though you may feel more energized by being alone, it is important — and sometimes relieving — to remember that there is strength in numbers. For some introverts, the apprehension in speaking and sharing is linked to the possibility of isolation or conflict once a thought is shared. As it relates to group dialogue, you might be pleasantly surprised to discover that there are others who think and feel as you do. Those folks may be more afraid or apprehensive than you to voice their ideas and opinions. That said, they may need your courage

and bravery to go first. You might be surprised to find that when you speak up, you have more support and agreement in the scenario than you anticipated.

For empaths, energy is palpable. Whether the feeling is exhilarating or unpleasant, being porous to the flow of other folks' energy comes naturally. Bravery for an empath may mean facing the discomfort of balancing your heart with your head. Here are three quick tips for those whose natural gift is empathy:

1. *Sort facts versus feelings.* High sensitivity is an exceptionally powerful energetic experience. While perception is reality, you must be mindful that strong emotions can easily become biases that impact behaviors. Be mindful and clear about what is real versus true.
2. *Distinguish between your stuff versus theirs.* For the sensitive souls who are new, unpracticed, or ungrounded with respect to the empathy temperament, the emotional lines can get blurry, and it may become hard to distinguish between where an outside person's feelings stop and where yours start. Implement practices that calm you down and clear your mind, body, and spirit so that you know when you are (still) carrying the energy and emotions of other people.
3. *Speak truth to power; help heal the room if you can.* While others negotiate within themselves whether to speak or not, you are additionally balancing how everything and everyone feels. When there is discord, the tension can become unbearable. Should you be grounded and regulated enough to do so, it may be your role to use your gift to aid dialogue participants in noticing and processing their feelings. You may be uniquely positioned to calm a space so that the moral imperative and the highest desired outcome of the conversation can take place.

Green Light: Go Forth and Be Great

How much better could conversations and experiments in human engagement be if we maximized our potential in how we showed up and expressed ourselves? Consider how much better communication would be if our behaviors brought out the best in others. Imagine a pattern of culture in human systems where our communication styles and temperaments were leveraged for good and not evil. How much more could we accomplish before, during, and after conversations if we had knowledge and acceptance of all the possible gifts, talents, and abilities in the space? When we are at our best and treated in a way that affirms our value, our ability to be awesome advocates, educators, supporters, and healers becomes boundless.

There are likely endless amounts of ways humans are supernaturally designed to exist and communicate on this planet. We need constructive criticism and introspection on how we are wonderfully yet challengingly made. It is also important to celebrate differences and their benefits to environments when we choose to grow and when we make spaces safer, braver, and more courageous. For the temperaments referenced in Ask #5, gratitude is extended for their following roles and benefits:

Extroversion naturally takes up a little more space than intended in conversation. This temperament is a well of words, and it knows how to use them. However, when they pause and listen, those with this superpower are incredible advocates who can be fearless in speaking up for others. In between sharing space with Ask #5 recipients, the person harmoniously empowered with extroversion will ensure communication is epic and action oriented.

Introversion naturally fades into the background and likes it that way. When we come back to keepers of this temperament for reconnaissance and wisdom deposits and the magic moment of their sharing happens, the rest of the room discovers that the individuals best designed to gather, disseminate, and translate highly detailed information are our quiet friends. People poised for introversion are recipients of patience and grace, and they will ensure that communication is thorough and complete.

Ambiversion selects its communication pathway based on the temperature of safety present (or absent) in a room. Sometimes this temperament needs a little Ask #5; sometimes it doesn't. Imagine, then, the greatness of an ambivert who leans into the bravery and courage to pull from its range of perspectives and preferences. They are guaranteed to be what the room needs and equipped to fill in the gaps so that nothing falls or fails. The charming soul-wielding ambiversion possesses the choice of whether to voice or not, which will ensure communication is balanced in expression.

Empathy is preeminent for the beings who take care of the soapbox speakers and the wallflowers. If efficiently, effectively, and emotionally regulated, the best person designed for the role of caregiver in communication and conversation are the empaths. They may not need to receive more time and space for composure and contemplation as much; however, they will be fully tapped in and know when it's time to come back to someone. Their "spidey sense," used properly, ushers in a healing component to any space. A guru of grounded empathy will ensure that all communicators in human spaces are seen, heard, felt, and affirmed.

When complications in communication surface, we may feel unsafe. Fear and discomfort increase our susceptibility to fall back into unhealthy coping strategies like hypervigilance and dissociation. Becoming paranoid may result in our seeing or sensing issues that may not be present; on the other hand, going numb causes us to miss seeing and feeling important points of connection. Pausing, as reflected in Ask #5, Come Back to Me, is an acceptable and self-care affirming request. We can find time and make room for those who need it. It's OK to allow moments for regrouping and regulation. Ask #5's continuous practice of hospitality in welcoming our fellow human system partners over and over reminds us that we can all get our cadence needs met. Met needs make way for the courage of self-awareness. And the better we know ourselves, the better we can unify our temperament talents and treasures for the greater good.

CHAPTER 8

Ask #6
Respect the Process
of Learning the "Right" Language

Ask #6 is an invitation for us to respect the process of learning the "right" language. Our experiences and memories are powerful. We remember those who support us. We remember those who critique us. A positive human experience can fill us up, and a negative human interaction can deplete us. When we engage with others for a prolonged conversation or period, learning opportunities present themselves (similar to Ask #3, Practice No Judgment). A new statistic or fact. A new name. A new perspective. A new paradigm. Sometimes, the invitation is for us to be the teacher of this new thing. Other times, we are being asked to be students. In either seat, it is hoped that we will assume our assigned role with grace. All parties involved should remember that learning new information as well as learning to be in relationship with others—whether new or existing—is a *process*; it does not happen in an instant. Processes have peaks and valleys. They ebb and flow. Processes require a cadence and a bit of compassion to traverse the growth edges. When Ask #6 is requested it is safe to assume something new or less familiar has entered a shared space. How well or poorly we navigate "new" is up to us.

What is meant by "the right language"? How can we determine what is ultimately right or wrong in the abstractness of words? It is easy for meaning and intent to be lost in translation. Few things are certain. In language and conversation, the more we know about a topic, the more accurately we can speak on it. However, it can take years to master something. Even then, heritage, art, music, literature, and pop culture reinvent themselves over and over, creating ongoing difficulties for interpretation. In an era of "cancel culture," it is increasingly easy to offend and make errors. When we feel confident about a topic, it may be easier to navigate conversations with others. One might assert they know how to select the most accurate terminology and feel equipped in approaching dialogue with the right language about the subject matter in which they have invested the greatest knowledge, time, and attention. In consideration of Ask #6, "right" language entails that we have an awareness that words matter and that we have an expectation that the most suitable words will be used in a given situation. How we speak about someone or something involves the creation of safer spaces as well as awareness regarding the specificity of the words we choose to use.

An example of the impact of words is the variety of verbiage used to describe the race and ethnicity of people who are US residents and ancestral descendants from the continent of Africa. Below is a timeline of the origin of when race terms first took root in common usage throughout history to describe and categorize humans with African ancestry:

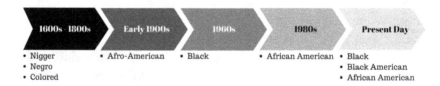

1600s–1800s	Early 1900s	1960s	1980s	Present Day
• Nigger • Negro • Colored	• Afro-American	• Black	• African American	• Black • Black American • African American

Current and acceptable terminology to describe said folks might be *Black, Black American,* or *African American.* The term *African American* emerged in the 1980s, and *Black* was popularized in the 1960s. Before *Black* was an acceptable term, *Afro-American* was used. Within the two centuries of the 1600s through the 1800s, written documents note use of the terms *negro, colored*, and, of course, the heinous term *nigger*. *Negro* was acceptable . . . until it wasn't. *Colored* in the United States lost its popular usage and approval by the early 1900s. (However, *People of Color* has been and is still an accepted term to refer to people with African heritage and lineage as well as to other people who do not racially identify *as white*.) Keep in mind, too, that *colored* is not to be confused with *people of color. Colored* also means something entirely different in South Africa than it did and does in the United States. And how would you racially categorize an immigrant from an African country who lives in the United States? Are they African or African American? And did you know there are some African nationalities who racially identify as white?

So, which term, obviously excluding racial slurs, is the right term to refer to someone with African ancestry? While there seems to be a continuum of more and less appropriate terms from which we can select for racial identity links to African ancestry, "right" in this instance is subjective. We may be required to go through a process to navigate intercultural spaces competently when trying to recognize and honor Black and African folks' culture the right way while avoiding overcategorization of people into one monolith.

As this example demonstrates, there are so many ways to get language and intention wrong. The right wording in human engagement is often subjective. The most correct answer in considering how to identify the most appropriate (or least offensive) phraseology is "it depends"—on situations, circumstances, preferences, and personal stories. The process of identifying the "right" wording and language is part of why Ask #6 matters in creating safer spaces.

Red Light: What to Stop, Look, and Listen For

The more confident and accurate one feels about a topic, it is assumed the less likely they are to be corrected or harshly critiqued when they speak about it. It is not easy to earn the title of subject matter expert. Further, it is harder to establish a relationship where we are comfortable enough to tolerate and withstand corrections from another person without being personally offended. Relationships that permit constructive critique, feedback, and criticism are likely bonds that have existed for a long time or exist in relationships that are more than transactional. Our mastery of knowledge and how we police said knowledge with others can extend beyond conversation and can dictate the relationship dynamics beyond feedback and correction. Simply stated, here are two ways that Ask #6 goes wrong:

1. *Afraid to be wrong.* Respect is a form of treatment we all wish to receive. Respect, however, is person specific. Being perceived as someone who knows what they are talking about is one way we seek to feel respected. Few people like to be told or treated as if they are wrong. Being critiqued is difficult. It can elicit feelings of doubt in our worth and value. It can be a cruel bedfellow to imposter syndrome. At its worst, being told or managed as if you have made a mistake feels like judgment. For some, being perceived as wrong speaks to signs of incompetence.

2. *Need to be right.* There is power in information. There is power in being right. Therefore, one can ascertain that being the source of the right information can give someone access to power and control. If you have the answers, you are in a great position to be the plug, the go-to, the point of contact, the right hand, and the lead. Explanations, expertise, and information dissemination in unsafe moments can be abused for defense attacks or even as perceived offense.

Practice Example: "In Denise's Defense ... "
Newlyweds Andrew and Denise started their daily evening walk in the still of night. It was an iconic starry evening, and the couple was grateful to have a moment of quality time together. Andrew broke the silence by asking his wife if he could share something that bothered him earlier in the day. In months prior, she had asked him to disclose more of his thoughts and emotions instead of holding things inside. Andrew believed a serene moment might be an ideal time to attempt to practice her request. Prior to sharing, he offered that his intention was to be forthright about disclosing his feelings and that he would wait for a better time to talk if Denise was

not in the right mood to receive feedback. Denise insisted he move forward with his communication. Andrew then disclosed—with carefully selected wording—how he perceived her management of a situation earlier in the day to be inconsiderate. Denise deemed herself to be a kind person; therefore, she took Andrew's feedback offensively and personally. She told him she was hurt and felt misunderstood. Though she agreed to listen to his thoughts and feelings objectively, she perceived that her character was being attacked and felt the strong urge to explain and defend her actions. As she talked, growing more passionate throughout her defense, Andrew sunk back into himself and regretted sharing. By the end of their walk, Andrew had become despondent. Denise was angry and confused as to why her husband was unwilling to reply and affirm the defense she offered for her earlier actions.

In the above example, both Denise and Andrew were afraid to be wrong. As the dialogue continued, Denise perceived an attack on her character and persisted in her need to be right by reclaiming power over her narrative through justification of her actions. This, in turn, disempowered Andrew's voice and exacerbated his fear of being wrong by incorrectly sensing the space was safe enough for him to share his feelings. Power and perception are often the highlands we must climb in conquering Ask #6, Respect the Process of Learning the "Right" Language. Traversing human systems is challenging in the best of circumstances. Now envision conflict and perception appearing as roadblocks on the route to information dissemination. Our hope is that we can reach the summit of communication and overcome its challenges. Regrettably, we may find that we choose hills to die on during rough dialogue when we force the issue of being right. We may also contribute to an exchange becoming less brave and courageous when we do not consciously disrupt out of fear of being wrong. Review some of the speed bumps and potholes along our journey to respect the process of learning the right language:

Embarrassment. Arguably one of the most painful emotions is embarrassment. Its anguish lingers far beyond the moment the transgression occurs. It seems to burn itself in our memories as well as the memories of others who may have witnessed the incident. We never seem to forget the moments when we have felt shame. The fear of embarrassment alone is a major barrier to the Nine Asks and gets in the way of us being safer, braver, and more courageous because the risk of embarrassment does not seem worth the reward of growth.

Inadequacy. A common complexity when overthinking how we show up in environments is feeling as if we are either too much or not enough. In either direction, a feeling of inadequacy or unworthiness takes over and causes us to behave in ways that are disingenuous. The feeling of being too much may make us stifle and silence ourselves. We may become afraid to be wrong and fail to speak up. When we experience a deeper feeling of not being enough, it may result in us taking up too much space with what we know to prove to others and ourselves that we are worthy.

Perfectionism. The more often someone is right, the closer they may implicitly or explicitly believe they grow near to accomplishing perfection. Some are not impacted by the temptation to be perfect and feel no pressure to perform for others. Others receive both validation and a dopamine hit when they are the recipients of A+ and 100 percent grades, both literally and figuratively. It is impossible to be perfect. It is unhealthy to strive for perfection. Invariably the chase for perfection will lead to disappointment. Additionally, perfectionism does not ingratiate oneself to others when the attempt to prove perfection takes place in shared spaces. It is an especially prickly character flaw if someone must be wrong so that you can be right.

Unrealistic Expectations. Expectations, especially when they are unrealistic, create many social dilemmas within human systems. We have expectations for situations and relationships, though often unknown to others. These unknowns usually lead to the expectations being unmet. One might liken an unrealistic expectation in human engagement to "script writing." Some will compose how they intend their engagement to be performed by themselves and with others. However, if no one else has the script except you, prepare to be disappointed. If we expect to be right, we may impose the expectation outwardly and hunt for opportunities to prove ourselves right. If we expect to be wrong, we may prepare ourselves to bypass discomfort through avoidance.

Power differential. Rank in relationship can imply power, and where there is more power, there can be an increased perception of being right. Some examples of power differential as it relates to Ask #6 may include but are not limited to parents and children, supervisors and subordinates, teachers and students, and law enforcement and suspects. Before any conversation occurs, these inequitable relationship dynamics often assume someone has power over another and a need to be right to maintain power. Meanwhile, their subordinate has the disadvantage of disempowerment and may fear being wrong. In these power dynamics, being wrong can be costly, and in the most extreme circumstances, it can be deadly.

Imposter syndrome. Have you ever gotten what you wanted and then felt fear or anxiety about being where (or who) you hoped to be? Perhaps the discomfort was due to your uncertainty of worth and value. Imposter syndrome is the condition of feeling doubtful and incapable of meeting expectations of success despite being objectively capable and competent. Imposter syndrome makes us feel undeserving or like a pretender. This condition shows up in several ways, including perfectionism, procrastination, project paralysis, and people pleasing (behaviors that have all been referenced as complications when practicing various Nine Asks). Notice when imposter syndrome causes you to take up too much or too little space in dialogue with others. A block in Ask #6, Respect the Process of Learning the "Right" Language, may be indicators that a deeper healing is needed inside of yourself to better manage interaction with others.

Defense mechanisms. We typically defend ourselves when we feel threatened and need protection. But what if statements such as "fighting back" and "defending myself" project a need to be right? Some people simply don't like being challenged or corrected. This posturing can activate behaviors threatening to Ask #6. Passionate conversations and energy-rich human engagement can sometimes have unintended impacts that make us feel unheard or as if our authority and perspective are being questioned. In turn, we may come to our own defenses and try to justify our points, even if no one is questioning us. Further, if we perceive someone as fighting back against us, we may go into survival mode and either respond with a fighting feedback loop or feel an overwhelming urge to flee or fawn by hiding and silencing ourselves. Either way, the results typically lead to the space feeling more threatening for everyone involved.

Yellow Light: Proceed to Practice with Caution

What if I told you we are always practicing Ask #6? Every time we are in conversation with someone—especially dialogue that ushers in opinions, information, or clarity—the opportunity will present itself for someone to be right and someone to be wrong or, at the very least, "spontaneously educated." Solid practices such as the following will hopefully result in learned behavior that will come in handy when we have the itch to be right or the anxiety of being wrong:

> *Understanding great versus good.* A wise senior leader once shared to her middle management subordinate, "Don't let the great be the enemy of the good." The worker bee paused, breathed deeply, and gave herself grace. This quote reminds us that aspiration has its place, but when we seek greatness and perfection without blemish or error, we might miss other elements that matter. Sometimes seamlessness and flaw-lessness—also recognized as a need to be right—are not the objective. Procrastination can defeat punctuality when we make room only for greatness. Correction can prevail over kindness when the operative goal is to be right. Know when the process is more important than the product.
>
> *Being right without being condescending.* Some of us grew up with elders who instilled in us the value of being a gracious loser and a humble winner. No one likes to be on the receiving

end of the negative energy that comes from sore losers and arrogant winners. Being right is not necessarily a prevailing indicator that a person will make a space feel less safe. However, the way in which one is right and educates others can have a profound impact on the culture and climate of a space.

Humbling oneself. Don't wait for external factors like shame, guilt, or embarrassment to force you to practice humility. Take it upon yourself to interrogate when you are being too big for your britches. Notice when you have the answers people need, but no one wants to receive them from you. Pay attention to times when the conversation feels hot but when the people with whom you are speaking feel cold. Can you tell when folks would rather be blissfully ignorant than torturously taught the right answer by you? Whether you are in the thick of human engagement with others or you are spending some quiet time alone, there is always room for humility.

Letting it go. Assume you are right again, just as you were right the last time. Correction may remind someone else of many other times when you have been right. Or maybe you remind people when you were correct. Are you the I-told-you-so person? Maybe someone is having a rough day, and they fumble over their words. Or perhaps the topic or language is a barrier to selecting the words that have the most meaning and matter the most for moral imperative. Human beings are not term papers to be graded and calculated for a summative score. We are all fallible human beings, even the folks who struggle to be infallible. At the end of the day, is it really necessary for you to be right and let others know that they were wrong? Did it make the space feel safer? Some things can and should be pardoned. Sometimes we just need to notice a thing and then let it go.

Green Light: Go Forth and Be Great

We all have some talent, gift, ability, or skill set that could be of value and use to others. These gifts may reside in your hands, your heart, or your head. Most have an awareness of their abilities. Some folks doubt that they have anything of value to share. We must believe that we have value whether we are exercising productivity or not. It helps us to believe that we have a responsibility to share what we know and that our knowledge is best communicated in a way that does not slight folks' integrity. Consider these offerings for compassionate contribution in human engagement:

Words matter. Approach and intentions matter. When we are convinced that there is felt safety in a space, we show up more authentically, which allows us to be at our best, as opposed to showing up on our worst behavior. At our worst, we can shrink and diminish the value of ourselves as well as others. When we are not operating in optimal condition, as we have discussed earlier in the book, the output suffers. Sometimes the output looks like business and workplace initiatives. Outputs could include the family structure. Included, too, is the integrity of learning and faith-based spaces. When we honor every voice as a wise contributor and know when to drop the proverbial microphone, our rising tide, in the words of President John F. Kennedy, "lifts all boats."

Constructive feedback is good. Someone you know protects and serves the written language by being the grammar police. They cringe when you mix up *their*, *there*, and *they're*. Heart palpitations follow when you incorrectly use *your* instead of *you're*. Though a slight blush of the cheek might follow, there is value in knowing when we are in error. Care about someone enough to not let them pronounce a word wrong or use it incorrectly in a sentence. Help a fellow human when they need insight or an outside perspective. Above all, guard yourself against the possible inflated ego when you get it right and get to educate and enlighten someone.

Take a leap of faith into leading. Leaders are expected to be right, and that can be scary or intimidating. Some folks who have not had the opportunity or desire to lead may seek assurance that they have enough competence, qualifications, and knowledge to contribute. Leaping in to lead with our voices is a gamble. Whether right or wrong, the deeper gain is trying something different. That's likely why the expression is called a leap of faith. In the natural, faith is complete trust or confidence. Supernaturally, it is often described as "the assurance of things hoped for, the conviction of things not seen" (Hebrews 11:1). Every now and then, pushing past the fear of being wrong and stepping into leadership requires a little faith (with no evidence things will work out) and hope and belief in our abilities and our purpose.

The act and art of introspection and reflection are important throughout the practice of Ask #6. If we notice we are already sensitive prior to entering into dialogue, Ask #6, Respect the Process of Learning the "Right" Language, will need extra effort to be effective. Hypersensitivity may cause one to seek or retreat from attention. If sensitivity grows during conversation, ego could result in outbursts. Heightened or triggered sensitivity could cause a potential speaker who's afraid to be wrong to turtle (back) into their shell and be mute. Sensitivity for the person who needs to be right may look like righteous indignation and a struggle with exhibiting humility. Sensitivity codes the brain to behave in whatever manner that gives folks the belief and experience of felt safety.

Wise leaders know that "If you're the smartest person in the room, you're in the wrong room." They invest in learning as a continual process. Periodically reflect on Ask #6, Respect the Process of Learning the "Right" Language, and assess why you need to be right and how you feel about being wrong. Be open to the possibility that someone else can help you grow and become a better version of yourself. If we're in the number one position, we may use being right as way to keep power. Power over others is unhealthy and corrupt. Power with others is healthier, but it is a process. It takes time, patience, and shared experiences to start nurturing a relationship with others where we both feel safe enough to help others—and ourselves—evolve.

CHAPTER 9

Ask #7
Take the Time to Listen First

Ask #7 is a request for us to take the time to listen first. Its desire is for people to feel and believe that they have the full attention of others when they are the storyteller. Because of the high frequency of transactional conversations that take place in human systems, we do much less active listening than we think. More times than not, we are waiting to speak. When leaning into this request of people, what they share is an awareness of what it feels like to be listened to and a desire to have the authentic attention of the person with whom one is speaking. Many speak of signs and patterns that inform them they are being heard — eye contact, leaning in, verbal fillers to affirm the listener is following the conversation, asking questions, etc.

Most human beings across all systems ultimately desire to be seen, heard, felt, appreciated, and affirmed. Listening is one of the most accessible and yet consistently difficult ways to practice recognizing the presence and the humanity of another. The act of listening is a demonstration of our ability to hold space for another human being. There are moments when we are helpless in being able to change the circumstances of another when they are in crisis. There are times when matters are brought to our attention and when we do not have the lived experience or the understanding to be able to listen empathetically or to be informed advocates and accomplices to change matters and circumstances. However, what we are all capable of is slowing down and being present for a person. Listening allows us, even for a small fraction of time, to do life with another person and to let them know that they matter enough to us for us to prioritize their story in the moment we have been called to listen and engage.

Sometimes we just need to get out of the way of the storyteller and allow them to speak and share freely, meaning long enough to relay the necessary information for our comprehension. We may find that questions and inquiries we have for the storyteller are answered before we ever need to ask the question. Taking the time to listen gives space, permission, grace, and allowance for a person to share (and course correct, if need be) their own words without modification or interruption. When we have been chosen as a recipient of a person's story, there is a responsibility for us—if we choose to accept our position as a listener—to be engaged. Remember we should ideally position ourselves as receivers of other's stories and believe the stories shared with us are gifts.

It may surprise us how often people of all ages feel erased or invisible during engagement because they were not listened to. Fully and actively listening honors the humanity of the storyteller. Without needing to know the perfect response, the perfect course of action, or the perfect next steps, one of the most important things we can do is let a person know, "I see you; I hear you, and, therefore, I honor you." We can do all these things simply by taking the time to listen.

Red Light: What to Stop, Look, and Listen For

Compassionate listening requires patience, which is a virtue many people spend a lifetime trying to improve. Providing a listening ear with an attitude of presence, patience, and benevolence (or a lack thereof) also can encompass our attitudes and can display transparency in how we value and manage the relationships and exchanges of folks with whom we are in conversation. One of the primary communication complaints folks have in all spaces is the feeling they are not being listened to. There may be an endless number of reasons why we sometimes stumble in offering Ask #7 to others. In addition to misreading our thresholds (Ask #2) as well as judgment (Ask #3), consider the following warning signs when our ability to take the time to listen first is met with adversity:

Interrupting. Interrupting is a primary complaint on how we drop the ball in listening to others. Interrupting happens for various reasons, including but not limited to excitement, a lack of impulse control, passion, and even cultural expression. Sometimes people interrupt because they do not respect or honor you. Other times people interrupt simply because they had a thought inspired by something you said and blurted a reply. As listeners, we must practice strategies to remember what we need to say while *resisting* the urge to say it in the moment. And as storytellers, we must speak up. Speak up if being interrupted dysregulates you. At the same time, if interrupting is not a big deal for you as a storyteller, a little grace is always appreciated.

Distracted listening. Our human brains are doing way too much all the time. We have incalculable pieces of information flowing back and forth in our neuroreceptors, and sometimes it is more difficult than other times to silence the noise and focus. This is why there are master teachers who guide folks in mindfulness meditation. We even struggle listening to ourselves. Watch for times when your head is so busy that it's hard for you to listen to anyone else.

Offering mindless (versus mindful) feedback. Can flat responses make people feel as if you are not listening? Mindless or unconscious verbal fillers in a conversation, such as "uh-huh" and "yeah," are not specific, decisive, and detailed ways for us to communicate to storytellers that we are actively listening to and able to reflect on what they share with us. The activity of listening and having an exchange of energy and information between a storyteller and a listener should also be person specific. If we are to respond, the response should be thoughtful and catered specifically for the storyteller with whom we are in conversation.

Providing radio silence. No response when a response is expected or requested is a very sensitive and touchy topic, including and especially for LGBTQ voices, BIPOC voices, immigrant and refugee voices, and other voices that are not in the perceived power majority. They often bleed out their stories, pains, and traumas only to be met with radio silence. We cannot ask people to be vulnerable in sharing their stories, believing, and perceiving that we are doing a good job of Ask #7, and then when asked to respond, we have nothing to say. No reply or response is often perceived and received as if we did not listen or we did not care.

Being dismissive. When the room is not familiar with uncommon speakers having the spotlight, they may check out or shut down when the storyteller is speaking. There is no set rule, criteria, or rubric for who gets to be a storyteller and who must be a listener. Storytellers are often the people we expect to be at the podium and on the stage. When we consider elements of justice, however, there is an increasing need for credible storytellers from all walks of life to be positioned on these same proverbial stages. When we do not respect the storyteller, we violate Ask #7, Take the Time to Listen First, because we dismiss their rank, worth, and value.

Stonewalling. A refusal to communicate or an intentional and conscious withdrawal from conversation is a jarring and threatening way to weaponize presence when the expectation is to take the time to listen first. Should the storyteller desire or request feedback or reflection, a refusal to speak or respond may be perceived as threatening and definitively an unsafe response once someone has shared their story. We, in some cases, have turned storytelling and conversations into political agendas and power dynamics. It is time to restore the mindfullness behind communication and to be much more present in how we show up for and with others.

Yellow Light: Proceed to Practice with Caution

Imagine all the prep work has taken place. You have researched every element possible. You have put hours of listening practice into place. You have studied, contemplated, and reflected on every possible outcome to prepare yourself for the big moment. Then an opportunity presents itself for you to take the time to listen first. What steps can you take to prepare for receiving someone else's story graciously? When we assume the responsibility of listening to someone's thoughts, ideas, concerns, questions, and grievances, consider balancing these natural human instincts:

Ego. Ego puts us in an undesirable position of defaulting to center our own stories. Even when we are listening to other people, it takes conscious thought to remove ourselves from focus and to center other people for an extended period in conversation. Sometimes our attention slips from keeping others in central focus and we go back to what we know — ourselves. Apart from folks who are struggling to be the main characters in their own stories due to people pleasing, ego has a wicked way of ruining our ability to take the time to listen first.

Power. Those who are in positions of power may struggle as listeners with Ask #7's request to take the time to listen first. Great listeners yield their privilege and power and allow the storyteller to be the most powerful person in the moment of conversation and engagement. If you get more talk time than the average person, listening might feel like writing with your less-dominant hand. For some, it is a very difficult ask to expect a powerful person to relinquish their throne and allow someone else to be in the spotlight. Consider this an invitation to practice empathy and to develop a new and much-needed skill set.

Time. One of the most frequently stated barriers and complications to Ask #7 is time. No one has enough of it. There are never enough hours in the day to accomplish all we desire to do. We do not even make time for our own personal interests. Therefore, it is a common experience to resist giving enough time and space for someone to share their story without rush or interruption. We may allow for a few minutes for someone to debrief. We hold space, but it might be while we're walking to the next meeting. We listen to children speak, but we don't stop working on tasks while they're talking. When thinking about time in a linear way, there will never be enough of it for us to justify freezing everything for an undefined moment of full presence for someone else to share their story and emotions. It must be a choice.

Emotions. There is an activist named Lee Mun Wah who discusses a concept he created called the privilege of numbness. In this framework, he describes moments and times when a story-teller is sharing their story and when the listener "responds" by pivoting and inserting their own narrative because they cannot relate to the storyteller. Instead of seeking to understand, they shift the attention back to themselves and are effectively void of feeling or numb in empathy. Conversely, there are times when folks are listening to someone's story and they become so overwhelmed with emotion, whether the emotion be rage, sadness, surprise, or intrigue, that their inability to manage their emotions becomes a detractor from the storyteller in sharing their story.

The five f's. There may be instances when we have been invited to take the time to listen first and in doing so, either the story, the storyteller, or environmental circumstances allow fear and discomfort to slip into a space. Once this occurs, often one of our five *f*'s will take over, as our body perceives that help is needed to aid us in surviving an experience. It becomes increasingly difficult, if not impossible, to fully, presently, completely, and actively listen to someone if you are in fight mode, if you desire to flee or run, if you are frozen, if you are giving in and giving up (fawning for self-preservation), or if your amygdala is seeking to align itself with whatever the group of people around you and the storyteller are doing to survive. The activation of any of the five *f*'s is a likely indicator that you have reached your capacity in listening and have no more to give.

"Thank you for coming to my TED Talk." When attempting to relate to something a speaker has shared, a listener may attempt to show relationship to the topic and inadvertently transform their turn to speak into a soliloquy or soapbox moment. Feedback loops are good practices in demonstrating

active listening. However, when a listener switches into speaker role and dominates the engagement with their own stump speech, the dialogue has lost its harmony and balance. Though good intentions could be at the root of the behavior, the absence of awareness and repositioning of oneself as the center of attention is a quick way to make a conversation feel less safe.

Practice Example: "Patience When the Teenager Is Texting"
Miguel came home from school emotional and exasperated. His mother, Minty, was finishing up some graduate school homework when she heard the front door slam shut. The pubescent middle schooler had obviously reached his limit after a bad day and was bubbling with pent-up emotions. Minty initially planned on admonishing Miguel for slamming the door. Then she recalled the many moments during her own difficult childhood when she was dysregulated and attempted to signal to her mother that she needed a listening ear and a shoulder to cry on. Typically, Minty's mother's response was to dismiss her feelings and share her own hardships to demonstrate to Minty that back in her day, life was so much harder. After the parable, her mother would often give Minty advice like, "That's nothing to cry about" or "Just focus on your schoolwork." Minty wanted to do a better job being present for Miguel.

Minty approached her son, who by now was in his room, lying on his bed. "Miguel, I heard the door slam when you got home from school. Are you OK? What happened?" He stared at the ceiling with his hands folded behind his head and replied dryly that he didn't want to talk about it. Minty softened her voice and affirmed to her son that she understood. She offered, "If you're open to writing or drawing your thoughts, you can text me." Miguel turned his head slightly to his mother whispering, "OK." "Let me know if you need anything or if there's anything I can do to support you," Minty extended as she left her son's doorway. Before she got to the bottom of the steps, her phone chimed; it was a text message from Miguel. For nearly an hour following, Miguel sent his mother text messages sharing little by little what happened and why he was so upset. Careful to not scare him away from sharing, Minty replied with brief affirming comments and acknowledgment of his feelings, only offering advice *after* Miguel was through sharing and requested her insight. After the flurry of messages stopped, Miguel quietly made an appearance in the kitchen where his mother had returned to her studies. He gave Minty a lingering hug and thanked his mom for listening to him.

Taking the time to listen to someone first and waiting to see if any additional action is needed is such a meaningful yet simplistic way to make a space feel safer. There is no rush in the pacing. There is a clear communication that the storyteller and their voice is valued. Great listening is supported by the appropriate virtuous applications of passion, wisdom, prioritization, and belief. These practices, examined below, aid in demonstrating worthiness of a storyteller to be the recipient of our time and attention when we are entrusted with the privilege of hearing what they have to say:

> *Passion.* When channeled appropriately, passion allows us to engage in practicing empathy for our storyteller. Being fired up, excited, angry, or enraged as a listener isn't necessarily a bad thing as long as we are careful not to allow our passion to overshadow the enthusiasm of the storyteller. A passionate and affirming listener will assuredly make the commitment to perform Ask #7 correctly and take the time to listen first. It is hopeful that our passion demonstrates itself in a way that is for the good of people with whom we are in contact. Misty used the passion of her negative experience with her mother to center her son, Miguel, in his story sharing. In this instance, her passion for her son and his hurt allowed her to be present and take the time to listen to him before rushing to respond to or repair his pain.
>
> *Wisdom.* Often, human engagement dialogue is between folks who are on different levels of position and power. It could be a parent and a child, a teacher and a student, a health-care provider and a patient, or a business leader and a client. When the person in the position of power has been sought out for conversation, it is often, but not always, assumed that a story

recipient will provide insight, information, and subject matter expertise. It can be difficult for people in positions of power and authority to listen for the sake of support (or just for the sake of listening) because they have been trained to listen for the purpose of advisement, caregiving, or problem-solving. Misty had the experience, wisdom, and presence of mind to simply be present for Miguel and to let him lead in what he needed from the dialogue experience. Misty's approach was spot-on.

Prioritization. In many more situations than we care to admit, we are the centers of our universes. That said, when we are called on to hold space, listen, and be in dialogue with another person, their voice must be the most important voice until they are done speaking. Even when we believe we have an amazing gem to share, a great listener defers and yields their own voice so that others have full space to speak. Folks who take the time to listen first have a way of making the storyteller feel as if they are the most important (if not the only) person in the world. Minty gave Miguel her undivided attention, and he returned the prioritization with his appreciation. Practice prioritizing those who speak with us as our number one focus.

Belief. Perception is reality. When a story is shared with us and we are asked to take the time to listen first before speaking, judging, or solving a problem, a deeper thing that is being asked of us is to believe the storyteller. Those who select us to share need to trust that their words are worthy of the time and attention we are giving them. We may have no idea if the information shared with us is 100 percent accurate in the moment. Frankly, that may not be our business or our role to decipher if we are listening *first.* Most often, our only job as listener is to be still, be quiet, be thoughtful, be mindful, and be receptive of the information as fact unless or until we have a reason to doubt it. Minty didn't need to interview Miguel's friends to fact-check his story. Miguel valued that his mother believed him. In doing so, she likely fulfilled one of his primary human needs.

We are human, and we are imperfect. Sometimes we get things wrong. Sometimes we mess up. Sometimes we fumble. So, watch for the following items, but don't obsess over them. Listening is difficult. No one is a perfect listener. Recall that when we know better, we do better. Here are some helpful things to know when practicing Ask #7.

Ask the person what they need. One amazing tool that can change the trajectory of how a conversation goes from the very first sentence is to set the intention. When a person communicates that they would like to speak with you, ask them if they need you to listen for the sake of listening or to listen with the intent to give advice. If you know what is expected of you as a listener and if you can be obedient and in agreement with what is expected of you, practicing Ask #7 will go much more smoothly.

Gauge your capacity to listen. The truth is both storytellers and listeners are whole people. We are messy. We are complicated. Sometimes we have bad days. Sometimes we are not in the mood to be great. Sometimes the Asks will be hard to do. As you pay more attention to yourself and your needs, you will have a better understanding of what your capacity level looks like from day-to-day and moment-to-moment. If you happen to be approached to listen to someone and if you know you are near, at, or beyond capacity, it is OK to communicate that you may not have the capacity to be a great listener in the moment. Pay attention to the times when you have what it takes to be a good listener and the times when you don't. Make sure to communicate to your storyteller so that they have choices and options regarding who and where to give the gift of their story.

Listen with your whole body. Earlier in this section, we lightly touched on demonstrative ways to let people know we are listening. What are small things you can do to let someone know that they have your full attention? Are you comfortable with eye contact? Are you able to repeat something your storyteller said to you with accuracy? Do you have insightful questions? Are they comfortable with touch if you are listening and reach out to touch their arm, shoulder, or hand? Are they (or you) comfortable with a hug after listening to their story? Allow your body to be engaged in the process of listening. Make sure that you have an awareness of how your body shows up and that it does not disrupt the activity and process of listening.

Be prepared to do nothing but hold space. Reflect on some of your heaviest moments in your life when you needed a friend, parent, or partner to support you. In your time of need, reflect on how they showed up for you and what they did for you. You might be surprised, or not, that much of what we need from others in moments when we feel low or in despair is a listening ear. That's it. There is conversation floating in social science spaces that asserts all we need when in crisis is eight minutes of a friend listening to us. Eight minutes doesn't seem like enough time to save the world (unless you are a super-hero). However, a few minutes of simply listening and noth-ing else can change someone's life.

Don't take it with you. One of the greatest risks in being a habit-ual good listener, and most especially being an empathetic listener, is that you will carry the weight of the gifted story with you and on you. It is good practice when performing Ask #7, Take the Time to Listen First, to know what practices, strategies, and routines must be a part of your life to keep the essence of a person's love but to shed the shadows of stories that don't belong to you. Those who show up frequently as listeners of others, such as service workers in community or caregivers in personal and professional spaces, often take on too much and confuse their stress with the stress of others. Make sure there is a clear delineation between your weight and someone else's weight. Simply put down the heaviness that does not belong to you. It does not make you a bad person. It makes you a practitioner of great self-care.

Green Light: Go Forth and Be Great

Just as with all the Asks, a little bravery goes a long way in us better demonstrating and practicing how to make spaces safer, braver, and more courageous for ourselves and others. The bravery desired and required to be a better listener includes internal values, virtues, and practices. It takes time to be a practiced and sustainably just listener. The mastery of active listening aids in creating opportunities for flow of human engagement that may have great dividends, such as:

Creating an opportunity for enlightenment. There's something magical about having aha moments. Epiphanies are lifelong opportunities for us to expand. From the moment we enter the world to the moment we transition out, we are given moments to open ourselves up to discover something new through the story of someone else. Listening creates access points for us to grow and evolve.

Connecting and engaging. Though some of us would like to believe we are loners, human beings inherently desire to connect and belong. Done the right way, Ask #7, Take the Time to Listen First, gives us a foundational level to be able to connect and engage with other human beings. The world can seem so dismal and hopeless. The simplicity of a conversation where both folks are leaned in to being gracious storytellers and responsive listeners can aid us in seeing ourselves in each other and grants the potential to form links and bonds.

Affirming someone else. There is a cliché that advises us to give flowers to the living, meaning that we should appreciate and value people in the present moment. How often do we think positive things about people but never openly and verbally articulate compliments to them? A positive thought can't plant a seed in a person's soul if they are unaware that the thought exists. Positive feedback, appreciations, and affirmations can make a person's day brighter. Your good news may be the only affirmation a person receives in a day. When we take the time to listen first, that simple act alone may be a way of affirming someone and letting them know they matter.

Showing up for someone. We have all had moments when we felt alone, isolated, disconnected from others, and unworthy of belonging. Some have had such hurtful experiences in life that they have an expectation of being disappointed. When we practice the Ask #7, Take the Time to Listen

First, especially when a person is in crisis or distress, it provides us the opportunity and the blessing of showing up for someone when they needed help. What greater gift is there than to be someone else's blessing in a moment of need?

We may have ideas and memories about when we performed the act of listening right and when we got it wrong. Do you know where your weak areas are? Do you know what you need to work on? Do you know what's difficult for you when you are in the listening seat and why it is difficult for you to listen? Are there certain people that are harder for you to listen to? Are there particular stories that are hard for you to hear? Instead of being hard on ourselves when we have fallen short of any of the Asks, including Ask #7, put the practices in place to be a better listener. Move forward by doing the right things on purpose.

CHAPTER 10

Ask #8
Grant Permission to Go Deeper or Decline

As we venture into conversations with individuals, a moment may come when it feels as if there's a page missing from the story to which we are listening. Information may become incomplete or unclear and, subsequently, hard for us to follow along or focus on. In this moment, we have a couple of different options. We can either decide and author for ourselves how the rest of the story goes (which would be a violation of Ask #4, Honor Confidentiality) or ask for more information to gain context and deeper insight, which the speaker may offer or decline to provide. A request for permission to go deeper is an indicator that someone is interested in learning more about the storyteller. Similarly, when we are creating safer spaces for ourselves and others, it is imperative that we pay attention to the state of our own beingness and our needs. Ask #8's other half, Grant Permission to Decline, honors that people may have moments when they do not have the desire, interest, or capacity to open up more. Let's explore how Ask #8 works.

There are a multitude of reasons why one might ask for permission to go deeper. If we are uncomfortable or unclear, it may be important to ask for more information from the storyteller. But exactly what is the reason we seek to know more? If we believe the story sharing may have an element of falsehood, we may seek more information to find the true north in what is being told to us. Other times, we are in a position of ignorance, and the only way to learn, unlearn, or relearn is by seeking more information from the storyteller. We, as recipients of stories, have a shared responsibility to comprehend a story correctly. Our responsibility is to ensure what we hear is understood and coherent. We do not have the right or authority to assign meaning from our own creation and insert it into someone else's story. Ascribed meaning leaves the integrity of stories unprotected. The Grant Permission to Go Deeper or Decline Ask creates the opportunity for us to protect ourselves and others. When a speaker is misunderstood, it presents a threat to safety. Comfort comes with being understood and with understanding others. When we feel comfortable and possess solid comprehension of the message, we minimize distraction and increase the likelihood that we will be better listeners. Great listeners are better able to focus on the speaker instead of themselves and their own feelings in the moment.

Ask #8 matters because people deserve to determine when they want to open up and share more of themselves—or not. In various kinds of spaces within human systems, people are sometimes pressured to divulge personal information. The pressure of obligatory confession exists in more spaces than Catholic churches. People must have the authority to decide if and when they choose to give more. Of course, there are always extenuating circumstances to which the Nine Asks do not neatly apply. Mandated reporting insists on compulsory sharing. Other legal situations require orders instead of asks. However, whenever we receive an *invitation* to make a space safer, braver, and more courageous, we should seek actions to do the right thing. Getting out of the way of a person's agency matters.

Red Light: What to Stop, Look, and Listen For

Anticipating discomfort or suffering about things that have not yet happened is better known as fear and has so much to do with why Ask #8, Grant Permission to Go Deeper or Decline, is hard. When we are in conversation with folks whom we either do not know or do not trust, the uncertainty can usher in hypervigilance. Skepticism and doubt can override our ability to find comfort in human exchange. If we perceive threat in a person's behavior, presence, or story, it will become increasingly difficult, if not impossible, to make a safer connection. In fact, our brains will convince us to believe that our suspicions are what keep us safe. Let's unpack discomfort-related hard stops that interrupt Ask #8's momentum when getting to know others better:

Rejection. The anticipation of rejection prevents us from being curious about other people. What is there to be afraid of? A lot! We may fear someone will assume negative intent behind our inquiry. "Why do you want to know? It's none of your business!" they could suspiciously retort after we request for permission to ask more questions of our storyteller. In truth, though, a person has every right to reject our ask and say no.

Depth. We are uncomfortable giving and receiving our deep thoughts, feelings, and emotions with other people because then we must contend with other people's unpleasant feelings and emotions. Often, we do not know what to do with our own deep feelings. Apart from empaths, we often do not know how to respond to the deep feelings of others. We often feel safer when the conversation remains at surface level. In the absence of probing, no one is expected to emote, and no one is expected to be responsible for other people's emotions. Unfortunately, discomfort with depth distances us from the ability to truly connect.

Dishonesty. Dishonesty might happen by omission or sometimes even by grand gestures of deception. The hint of being lied to conjures up a plethora of negative emotions and usually stirs up challenges we face regarding trust. Some avoid asking for permission to inquire for more details because they fear the answer on the other side of the question will be deceitful. Some fear that stepping into an inquiry for more information will lead to disappointment regarding Ask #1, Be as Honest and Vulnerable as Possible.

Sometimes the block to Ask #8 isn't discomfort but rather a lack of capacity. Clear perspective is invaluable, but it takes effort to harvest enough information to gain solid understanding. Too little information can be a barrier that prevents us from seeing, hearing, and perceiving messages clearly. We don't want obstructions blocking our views or access. The virtue of having understanding appreciates full, uncompromised perspective in someone's story. That may not be automatically given. We might have to request the unabridged version of a story in order to understand, and we may simply not have the capacity for more. Here are some ways capacity (or lack thereof) prevents progress in our ability to ask for more details during story sharing:

People-pleasing. The desire to satisfy and please other people can get in the way of enacting Ask #8. However, asking to go deeper in conversation could be considered an act of conscientious disruption in our normal ways of engaging with one another. If your sole objective as a listener is to satisfy someone else and you have little capacity to handle ruffling feathers, your coping strategies could prevent you from submitting a question that needs to be asked. People-pleasing may also get in the way of how you embody per-mission to decline. If you believe declining the request to go deeper will offend others, you might say yes to requests that should be refused. People-pleasing nullifies the practice of the Nine Asks because there is no authenticity behind it.

Shutting down. Powering off during Ask #8 can be a tremendous barrier in our efforts to create safer spaces. When we shut down conversation, inquiry, and curiosity, we threaten the access to connect. For some, shutting down is a strategic measure and is done deliberately. For others, the shutdown may be connected to overwhelm and burnout. It is an important warning sign that capacity is compromised and that a space has the potential to be unsafe.

Ignorance. We don't know what we don't know. We cannot blame people for lacking knowledge they were never offered or taught. It is difficult, too, to blame folks for dif-ficulty in comprehending others' stories. However, the excuse of ignorance or unwillingness to ask demonstrates a lack of willful capacity to improve in Ask #8. Ignorance is not bliss if its impact creates harm in a shared space. Explore your capacity and desire to learn and know more. Feigning ignorance, especially if there is no attempt to rectify the mental state, is a significant threat to safer spaces.

Judgment. Sometimes assumptions and biases are unknown, surfacing only after we ask for permission to learn more about someone's story and then hear a detail that disrupts our core principles. Judging someone after asking them to share more is an egregious way to misuse or abuse someone's trust in the practice of requesting permission to deepen or to decline giving more information. Whether we refer to it as stigmas, assumptions, or plain ol' judgment, our values, beliefs, and opinions when in conflict with others often block our ability to go deeper, especially for the sake of creating connections and authentic relationships.

Temperament. Our energetic ways of communicating and showing up in the world can sometimes influence or interrupt how we seek more information and clarity about a person's story. It also impacts how we accept or reject a person's interest in getting to know more about us. An introvert may seldom seek or share more information because (extended) interaction with others depletes them. On the other hand, an extrovert may overshare by missing the cues that a person is not ready to deepen dialogue. Temperament and a person's natural higher or lower capacity to tap into deeper durations of human engagement could be a barrier to safer spaces.

Yellow Light: Proceed to Practice with Caution

Ask #8 reflects the element of the unknown. There is usually more information we do not know, and often, we are curious about increasing our access. When gaining access to more insight the wrong way, the communication climate gets messy quickly. It is possible that we are already in a relationship with folks whom we believe we know like the back of our hands. However, there may be more to them that lies beneath the surface. It is acceptable to seek more insight if the pursuit is done the right way and for the right reasons. Grant permission to go deeper with careful intention by building on your practice via the following don'ts:

Do not rush, push, or pressure people. If someone is not ready to share, we should not press the ask and force the issue. There are reasons why a person tells us no. "No" always communicates there is no consent, and that directive is to be honored. When permission is declined, it should not be received or perceived as a maybe or an opportunity for us to convince people to share when they are not explicitly comfortable doing so. That said, we also cannot decide in the middle of a storyteller's granting of our request for Ask #8 that they are taking too long to share their story. Individuals have a right to determine how, when, where, why, and to whom they share their story. If they do not trust the conditions provided, we must honor that and let it go.

Do not teach when you're tired. Permission to ask can be a very delicate invitation for those who are living in identities that have been othered or marginalized. They either are put in positions where they are invisible and never asked about their stories or are asked to share too often and the sharing of their story requires them to teach others who do not understand or have earnest interest in who they are and how they feel, especially when othered. This can be exhausting and can lead to burnout, which is sometimes why folks who belong to disenfranchised communities say no when asked to share more.

Do not decline in a rude way. Grant Permission to Decline, the second half of Ask #8, submits that there is authority on both sides of the request to know more. The storyteller always holds power and ownership in creating and sustaining safety in a space. If one is asked to share more about their story but they then examine their boundaries and thresholds and determine that they do not have the capacity or desire to do so, it is OK for them to say no. Declining a listener's request to go deeper is not necessarily an indicator that a space is less safe, unless their no is extended in a way that is harmful, hurtful, coarse, or curt, which sets the space back in being safer and braver.

Do not be nosy. Being nosy differs from showing curiosity. When we are being nosy, we are seeking a person's deeper honesty and vulnerability with no desire for understanding, relationship, or engagement beyond the moment. It is harmful for us to needlessly ask for more information. There is a difference between healthy curiosity, exploitation through spectacle, and being nosy when extending an ask to deepen sharing. Healthy curiosity demonstrates a desire for deeper understanding, relationship, or engagement. Seeking a spectacle makes someone the target of a joke, judgment, or exploitation.

The practice of obtaining permission to go deeper or decline relies on trust in good intentions, which takes some courage and consistency. When we develop some strength and muscle memory for seeking permission to go deeper, Ask #8 gets easier. Once you're in the practice of what not to do, then you can focus on what you should do:

Do accept no as a possible answer. Leaders aren't used to hearing no from subordinates. Caregivers and service providers are notorious for having poorly practiced boundaries, including denying others' requests. No is one of the simplest and most direct boundaries we can extend. While you may feel as if saying no to someone is being harsh, no is an acceptable answer and a full sentence. It is OK to say no, and it is a fair response to an ask we know we cannot fulfill.

Do determine if it's worth it to ask. Some information should be on a need-to-know basis, and every piece of someone else's information *isn't* something we need to know. Sometimes we're curious about information that will not improve the safety of the space or the relationship. A good practice is to assess if it is worthwhile to inquire for more. If it does not lead to a greater good for a space and the people involved, it might be better, as the expression goes, to leave well enough alone.

Do give context and trigger warnings before sharing details. Storytellers may feel inclined to share background details because the topic is complex and complicated. They have the right to share their story their way. It is acceptable for a storyteller to ask if it is OK to share context when going into more details. There may be familiarity and normalcy regarding distressing aspects of a story or talking points, but these same elements of a story could trigger someone else. Let someone know if there are parts of your narrative that could be difficult to hear, such as the trigger warning in the beginning of this book. This gives the listener the opportunity to decide if they would like to move forward in hearing more or if, based on their own boundaries and thresholds, they desire to rescind their inquiry.

Do engage enlightenment. Sometimes we want more information to prove a point, but in so doing, we may miss out on a great opportunity to learn a new thing or to connect with someone who can expand our minds. Interrogate for the purpose of illumination and prepare yourself for the possibility that growth is on the other side of Ask #8. Permission to deepen and seek insight might grant you the gift of more questions than answers.

Practice Example: "A Present No for a Future Yes"

Uncle Dan, as generations of folks in the community referred to him, was known for being incapable of transactional conversation. When he asked "How are you?" he waited for your real answer. Some loved the warmth of his genuine eye contact, hugs, and introspective prompts during conversation. Others who found discomfort in going deep avoided him at all costs when he made a beeline to greet them and check in. He was frequently invited to gatherings in his neighborhood to add elder wisdom and value, so Uncle Dan was naturally in attendance for the culminating reception of a special program that benefitted the holistic development of young men of color.

As attendees filled the small event space and funneled through the food buffet line, Uncle Dan made his rounds, catching up and connecting with past and present friends and mentees. Kyron, a young advocate in the community, caught Uncle Dan's eye. Kyron tended to be pensive but always cordial. Uncle Dan sauntered over to Kyron and greeted him with a toothy smile and belly laugh. The two men gave each other "dap," a colloquialism for a Black hand greeting and embrace. Uncle Dan made it through barely a minute of small talk before putting a hand on Kyron's shoulder and saying, "Brother, you've been busy this year! I've seen your work, and I'm proud of all you've been doing. I want to hear about the family, but right now, how are you doin'?" Kyron puffed his chest out slightly and began to give a generic, acceptable reply. As he spoke, Uncle Dan tilted his head, softened his eyes, and looked carefully back at the young man. "Brother, you're carrying a lot of weight. Do we need to do a real check-in?" Sheepishly, Kyron lowered his head with his shoulders and voice following. "I'm not gonna lie to you, Uncle Dan. I'm not OK. I don't wanna talk here, but can we meet up sooner than later to talk for real?" Feeling the gravity of his intuition, Uncle Dan quickly affirmed, gave Kyron another hug, and followed up with him days later.

The two ended up meeting semiregularly for conversations on mental health, relationships, and purpose. Uncle Dan often led the dialogue with lots of questions and followed Kyron's cadence on how he felt during each conversation, including what he was and was not ready to discuss.

Green Light: Go Forth and Be Great

The moral imperative behind Ask #8, Grant Permission to Go Deeper or Decline, should be grounded in understanding. Understanding does not imply agreement, nor does it imply acceptance. Understanding does not mean that a person is on your side or that you successfully recruited the listener into your school of thought. Understanding is a reflection of gained insight and clarity. Know when your intentions are—or are not—to simply understand or to be understood. It can make all the difference in the world in how you navigate a conversation with another person.

Opening up to someone is just the beginning with Ask #8. If we have positive intent and a good moral imperative for why we seek to gain more information, we are on our way to realizing some of the following numerous benefits of safe and brave spaces:

Deeper understanding. When we have a positive experience from asking for more information, sharing more information, or even giving a healthy no, it aids us in developing better trust for others and better trust within ourselves. The feeling of confusion about a person, place, thing, or idea can complicate our ability to engage and be present. When we positively grant permission to go deeper or decline, we can access a deeper understanding and better command of our surroundings. That advances the experience of feeling safer.

Internal connection. We drastically underestimate the necessity of having healthy relationships with ourselves. We often prioritize our external connections, but we must also have an internal connection with our own beingness.

Clarity. Even when the response we receive from Ask #8 are not the answers we desire, there is benefit in knowing where we stand and how to move forward. When we have clarity, it assists us in determining parameters for acceptance, expectations, and boundaries.

Self-advocacy and self-care. When we know we have stepped up and stood our ground—firmly planted—for our own benefit, it is a strength like no other. There's something special about stepping into our own power and fighting for ourselves. Ask for you. Accept or decline for you. The discovery, rediscovery, or actualization of finding and using our voices is an experience we all are worthy of pursuing.

The overall purpose of the Nine Asks is to create safer and braver spaces, enabling us to share more of our authentic selves with others. A key contributor to authenticity is the ability to be genuine and transparent about who we are. It does not ask for us to hide or code-switch for acceptance. Our stories and our power over them are our birthright. One challenge regarding unfinished storytelling is when the listener hears a portion of our experience, does not have the remaining portion of our story, but decides for themselves the narrative's trajectory. Stigmas and stereotypes (referenced in detail in Ask #3, Practice No Judgment) is an example of this. Accuracy in understanding others matters. It honors how a person defines their own reality. We are the only ones who have full and complete awareness of how our chapters end as well as their twists and turns. We are the only ones authorized to disclose more *if* there is more to be shared (see Ask #4, Honor Confidentiality). Asking and granting permission to access these deeper parts of our stories are essential for establishing safety as we seek true understanding of one another.

CHAPTER 11

Ask #9
Stay in Your Seat

Staying in your seat is about attentiveness and presence. It does not feel safe to talk to people who are not present — their bodies physically there but their minds and hearts checked out. Lack of awareness diminishes folks' ability to notice things that matter.

How many times have you been in a virtual meeting with your camera off and microphone muted? The absence of our face and voice lends itself to being mentally absent as well. You likely miss content when you are only partially present. Worse, you might not even care. We've likely attended countless meetings while busying ourselves by texting, emailing, or even drawing geometric doodles in the corners of the meeting agenda. When there is dialogue or conversation taking place, we are the intended audience. Yet, we are doing everything but focusing on the speaker.

Ask #9, Stay in Your Seat, matters because it implores us to not miss the moment. There is value in being present. When we are engaged in a space with other human beings, there is an invitation for belongingness and a collective consciousness we have been invited to join. Opportunities for collegiality and connection present themselves when we are awake, alive, and alert. Whether we inhabit an introverted or extroverted consciousness, there is value in the chance to build something with others or to experience the communal accomplishment of a shared task.

Red Light: What to Stop, Look, and Listen For

The world and all the specific spaces we inhabit compete for our attention. Meanwhile our internal communication is usually the contender that wins the battle. Let's explore the ways our minds, bodies, and spirits get in the way of us staying in our seats to be connected and engaged with others. We are only human. We miss things, and we make messes. The damage is not necessarily in the rupture; the more egregious error is not seeking to make repairs. If or when you rupture Ask #9 by not staying in your seat, it's likely the fallibility of human nature is to blame.

Think back to the chaordic path. When there is too much chaos, we are distracted and do not grow. Some of us never outgrow the dysregulation of overstimulated bodies and minds. Honestly and empirically, it is hard to be present. Various studies over the decades have been conducted to measure attention spans. Microsoft Corporation conducted a study in 2015 which found that humans have an average span of attention that lasts a mere 8.25 seconds.[3] (Goldfish can pay attention for 9 seconds.) We're learning and taking in new information from moment to moment. Our brains reward us with a hit of dopamine when we feed it new stimulants. Stimulants are everywhere, and it is hard to silence the urge. When there is too much order, we are bored and do not grow. Let's look at reasons why we struggle to be present:

Creature instincts. There is an acronym in the behavioral health-care industry known as H.A.L.T., which stands for hunger, anger, loneliness, and tiredness. H.A.L.T. represents the stressors we experience when we are unable to have our basic needs met. Think about standardized testing seasons for primary and secondary students. Picture staying in your seat for the SAT, ACT, or bar exam when your belly is empty, you started the morning arguing with a sibling, you have no friends, or you've been struggling with insomnia for weeks.

H.A.L.T. reflects four main warning signs that we are not OK and that we need to redirect attention to our physical and emotional health. Somatic ailments (e.g. pain, elimination, etc.) play second fiddle to no one and nothing. Creature instincts like H.A.L.T. keep us from staying in our seats. When we are stressed, our attention goes offline, and whatever was the most important thing outside of ourselves drops in priority.

Focus is not on me. We may not be the centers of the universe, but we as humans do struggle with how to balance a focus on others with a preoccupation for our own experiences. We may want to deny our gravitation to self-importance and self-obsession, but we are designed to think of ourselves and take care of ourselves. Sure, there are extremes to this notion. Too many times, we incorrectly label self-centered individuals as narcissists. At the opposite end of the continuum, people pleasers and caregivers, especially those whose stories are connected to trauma bonding and codependency, have a difficult time considering themselves at all. We cannot practice Ask #9 in a healthy way if we do not have an awareness of our own needs in a shared space, but it is hard to stay in our seats and focus on others when we are completely focused on ourselves.

Disconnect. When frustration sets in from not comprehending or misunderstanding, it can easily lead to shutdown. Whether the misunderstanding or lack of comprehension is based on a lost point or language that is lost in translation, it is a mental block and makes it that much easier for us to check out.

Multitasking. There is a not-so-secret society of people who belong to what is affectionately called "Team Too Much." These are folks who consistently multitask. They have places to go, people to see, assignments to finish, and errands to run. Their phones are constantly chiming with notifications of calls and text messages. They have emails to answer and meetings to attend. The world rewards multitaskers for chasing their unending list of things to do. However, the price paid for multitasking is usually effectiveness and quality. Our culture values productivity not presence. It is hard to pass up the opportunity to cross an item off the to-do list and instead give your time and attention to someone or something else.

Noise and distractions. Unless you have mastered the practice of mindfulness meditation, odds are high that your mind is noisy. Fire alarms. Slamming doors. Screeching tires. We can't control the unpredictability of the stimulants of the world. Mindfulness silences all noise and focuses exclusively on the breath that exists in the body. Conversely, a mind challenged by executive functioning disorders, such as attention deficit hyperactivity disorder (ADHD), struggles to silence noise and reduce chaos down to quiet hums. Imagine that our minds function like antennas for radio stations. A clear mind can focus on one station and tune in to be soothed by its sounds. A busy mind may attempt to listen to all radio stations that pass through its antenna, resulting in deafening static. Once the trance of focus is broken, it is extraordinarily hard to lock back in.

Intrusive thoughts and rumination thinking. Intrusive thoughts are described as unwanted thoughts and images that bring discomfort. They may take the form of thoughts that are unusual, bothersome, or hard to control. Rumination can encompass various forms of thought, including brooding, reflective, intrusive, and deliberate. The gravity with intrusive and ruminative thinking is that the thoughts get stuck in our heads and we cannot get them out. As much as we might desire to focus and stay present, the intrusive or ruminative thoughts prevail.

Invasive emotions. It is generally accepted knowledge that humans are born or wired with a minimum of six primary emotions, including joy, anger, fear, sadness, disgust, and surprise. Typically, an external experience evokes a feeling, and an emotion is the effect. We may begin a human experience fully engaged and focused; however, once an emotion is activated, whether it be from the storyteller or an outside element, it can be difficult to remain present and redirect the emotions to more constructive behavior and focus on the conversation, engagement, or task at hand.

Stress, trauma, burnout, and overwhelm. When we miss the signals our bodies issue to let us know the proverbial gas tank is running low, we can run out of gas unexpectedly. We often push ourselves to the limit, having no real gauge of the genuine limits of our capacity. It is impossible to stay in our seats when we have nothing left to give—even to ourselves. The sources of these signals are typically overloads of stress, trauma, burnout, and overwhelm. Two primary ways distress shows up and interrupts our ability to be present and focused are dissociation and hypervigilance. Dissociation causes us to shut down or disconnect from thoughts, feelings, memories, or sense of self. We go numb. Hypervigilance, conversely, is described as inaccurate information filtering that leads to enhanced sensitivity. A hypervigilant mind or behavior pattern may have exaggerated feelings and translate everything into warnings of eminent threat or danger. Emotional distress shifts us into survival mode, and once that is the primary focus, staying in our seats decreases in importance.

Negative spirit. You might refer to it as discernment, sixth sense, intuition, or the power of perception. We can sometimes pick up the energy of a room or a person's vibe. Those who are led by their spirit, sixth sense, or intuition often trust this voice more than any other. However, if the spirit communicates to a person with the gift of discernment that the energy is positive, said person or thing will have their undivided attention. If the spirit tells an intuitive person that the energy is off, focus is nearly guaranteed to shift away from the source of the perceived negative energy.

Practice Example: "Family Feud"

Leo and his daughter Leeza were having yet another sarcastic exchange about her outfit of the day during the family dinner. Leeza was a vibrant teenager who liked to experiment with her stylistic expression through clothing, hair, and accessories. Her father, however, was a straightforward businessman and preferred attire to be more casual and conservative. He was sensitive about appearances and reputation and didn't want her clothing to be louder than her scholastic aptitude. It was fairly typical for Leeza and Leo to have prickly conversations without causing much alarm to the rest of the family members. Usually during these conversations, Leeza's mother, Ariel, was checked out. Following the end of a workday, Ariel had a thousand things on her mind that did not include her husband and daughter's daily debate about makeup and wardrobe choices. Therefore, she typically had very little mental energy left to participate in any family feuds. Decision fatigue set in by about 7 p.m., and she had no capacity to choose sides on who the winner of the arguments would be.

One particular evening, the healthy debate and family joking went a little further than both Leeza and Leo intended. Leeza had had enough of being the source of her father's criticism and decided this would be the day she would stand up for herself. As the conversation began to escalate into a debate and then a full-blown argument, Leeza felt herself losing focus. The angrier she became, the stronger her impending headache and stomachache pounded in her body. Leeza's physical discomfort distracted her from being able to pay attention when her father was speaking, now more sternly than before. The less she appeared to be listening, the more Leo grew in his anger, believing Leeza's behavior and mannerisms were a sign of disrespect. The volume of voices increased and caught Ariel's attention. Scrappy squabbling signaled that she needed to tune in tonight and be present as a conscious bystander in the conversation. Soon enough, the exchange between Leo and his daughter trickled into unhealthy territory, and both began making personal attacks on each other's character. Thankfully, Ariel was paying attention now and had the presence of mind to notice that neither was OK. In fact, Leeza was on the brink of tears. Ariel knew at this moment both her husband and her daughter needed her to help them end what had become a very destructive conversation. She asked her husband, Leo, politely to leave the room and give her time and space alone with Leeza; he obliged. Ariel then wrapped her arms around her daughter and allowed Leeza to vent and weep in her arms until she grew tired and drifted to sleep. Once Leeza was resting and Leo also had time to calm down, Ariel reflected on the conversation with Leo and offered suggestions on how the family could better navigate future conflicts in a more mutually mindful way.

In the beginning of this family-feud scenario, Ariel was checked out of the conversation and not doing a good job of staying in her seat. She was neither connected nor engaged and therefore was ineffective in noticing how Leo or Leeza had approached the engagement. Father and daughter entered into the conversation present and positively engaged, but as the dialogue became decreasingly functional, their abilities to stay in their seats diminished. Though unaware of its onset, H.A.L.T. emerged as Leeza's warning sign that she no longer felt safe or brave enough to practice Ask #9 and stay in her seat. Fortunately, in this example, Ariel was able to re-ground herself, refocus her attention, and notice that the room needed her to bring her gifts to bear by rebalancing the space. Ariel's role serves as an example of the power of the bystander, particularly when conversations with positive intentions take a wrong turn. We never know when the climate will change and when our gifts will be needed to reestablish the Nine Asks. It is never too late to reintroduce safer, braver, and more courageous practices back into human engagement as long as folks in shared spaces care enough to repair the ruptures we sometimes create.

Also notice that several other Asks showed up in the above example. If Leeza would have been able to practice Ask #2, Respect Boundaries and Thresholds, quicker and more readily, she may have picked up on her emotional response and realized that she was not capable of having a functional conversation any longer. Leo was not cognizant of the fact that the jovial family conversation had slipped into a poor demonstration of Ask #3, Practice No Judgment. At some point when both Leeza and Leo neglected to keep their conversation above bar, neither was practicing Ask #6, Respect the Process of Learning the "Right" Language. Personal attacks are usually an indicator that ideal language has not been chosen in the verbal exchange. Ask #9, Stay in Your Seat, is a foundational example of how the application of multiple Asks are a best practice to aid human beings in their efforts to pursue being individually and collectively healthy, healed, and whole. In part 3, we will explore more about how the Asks work in tandem with each other.

Yellow Light: Proceed to Practice with Caution

Keep in mind the adage that declares, "Practice makes perfect." It is perhaps truer to say that "practice makes permanent." This is true for habits and hobbies; if practiced regularly enough, the behaviors will gradually become second nature. This is also true for our emotional regulation and interpersonal skills. What we do regularly can be reinforced and become our automatic responses in human systems and in human engagement. Reflect on the following suggestions in hopes that they can become good permanent practices of Ask #9 for you:

Prioritize. Prioritizing means identifying the most critically important items among a group. Make a list of everything you must do and everything you are responsible for in this moment. Evaluate the length of the list. Now, rank your items in order of importance. Is the person who wants your time and attention on the top of your list when they're speaking with you? When we are in dialogue, the person to whom we are listening is (or should be) the priority.

Prepare properly. Ask #9 requires you to quiet your body, mind, and spirit. The practice of staying in your seat may include expecting and accepting tension and discomfort. For some, the best possible practice to ensure you can stay in your seat and remain engaged is to prepare for the moment. If you know there will be tension or challenges when heading into human systems or engagement with people who will challenge you, it may be a good idea to set yourself up for success. Identify predictable problem areas. Consider what those challenging areas need. Know yourself and what you need so that you can be your best for whoever needs you.

Pray to speak and pause to listen. Consider the reciprocity that should exist in healthy communication. Reflect on your role when in a room. Even in spiritual practices, there is an exchange when we are fully present and stay in our seats. We pray to talk; then we pause to listen for the answer. When we co-create safer spaces through staying in our seats and being present, we can meaningfully engage in giving and receiving, praying, and pausing with others.

Green Light: Go Forth and Be Great

It is considered a noble practice during sitting meditation to notice but not engage the discomfort of your body, silence your mind, and solely be present with your spirit. Ask #9, Stay in Your Seat, is not a request for us to become masters of meditation. But similar principles apply as we stretch ourselves to improve our ability to sit still and stay in our seats for and with ourselves and others.

We make a conscious choice about how we spend our time and attention. Time is how we honor our ancestors and how we create the legacy that will come after us. We might like to keep all our excess time to ourselves and attempt to complete the impossible list of things we charge ourselves to do from day-to-day, but when we stay in our seats for someone, we communicate what we value. Making a conscious agreement to be in fellowship for a measure of time is a message of respect. It is virtuous to decide and commit to an exchange of thoughts and ideas.

The benevolent concepts of Sawubona and Shikoba from South African Zulu culture are perfect embodiments of what is possible when we get Ask #9, Stay in Your Seat, right. As a reminder, *Sawubona* means, "I see you," and its response, *Shikoba* means, "I am here." Together, the exchange between these two greetings communicates that, "Before you saw me, I did not exist." When we are present for and with each other, we bring each other into existence.

Note that *you* matter in this exchange. A safer, braver, and more courageous space requires *your* presence. It needs your identity, your quirkiness, your thoughts, your questions, and your consciousness. The room most especially needs those who have been othered and those who have been historically blocked from access. The room needs the ears of students and the voices of teachers.

Everywhere you go, you grace the room with your presence. But you represent so much more. You represent everyone who contributed to your successes. You represent dreams and prayers of ancestors who delight that you embody them. You represent elders who have faith in your ability to finish the good work they started. You represent the DNA of future generations who will attribute their safer spaces to you. All those whom we represent need us to stay in our seats and be present, and when it's time to stand up and move on, we can and will carry the energy of the safer spaces we build from one place to the next. Our practices enable us to be the personification of safer spaces. When we know better, we do better. We can be present in every environment we dwell in, including working spaces, learning spaces, living spaces, faith-based spaces, and our own selves. When we are present, we can transform rooms into manifestations of miracles. We can make life better for one another. When we allow the Nine Asks to change us, we can be a change agent in other spaces, and in every space, we can usher in more safety, more bravery, and more courage.

Most of us desire to believe there is meaning and purpose to our lives. Some know what they have been called to do. Others are still searching or waiting for the signs of their assignments. We seldom discover our purpose when we are checked out; we must be tuned in. There is a still, small voice that alerts us to our purpose, and sometimes the idea lightbulb flashes amid others' words and deeds. When people are compassionate, participative listeners who are focused on their storytellers, it is communicated that they matter and their stories matter too. We can receive and reciprocate that message with our attention as well. Just as a storyteller's story is their gift, a listener brings the gift of their full and undivided attention. Listening and presence are the *ideal* embodiment of Ask #9 — and, indeed, of all of the Nine Asks.

PART THREE
APPLICATION OF THE NINE ASKS

CHAPTER 12

Integrating the Asks

Now that we have explored the Nine Asks individually and in detail, let us consider the exercise of *practicing* the Nine Asks in real time. These invitations for the co-creation of safer spaces do not function in isolation of one another. In fact, they interplay with one another in a myriad of ways. Take, for example, Ask #2, Respect Boundaries and Thresholds: When we undertake Ask #8, Grant Permission to Go Deeper or Decline, it requires us to already be in practice of knowing and adhering to our boundaries and thresholds. We would not have knowledge or an internal compass of how to navigate an inquiry into our deeper stories without an understanding of our conditions for safety and limitations for stretching. None of the Nine Asks can be displayed in their fullness without the practice of Ask #1, Be as Honest and Vulnerable as Possible. A surface-level conversation has already omitted honesty and vulnerability, which assumes the other Asks cannot be genuinely honored. Ask #4, Honor Confidentiality, for example, is a moot point if one is not already practicing being honest and vulnerable. There is no need to seek permission for extended dialogue if there is no sincerity and transparency to begin with.

In moments of communication crises, use of the Nine Asks may help to navigate uncomfortable conversation. In most cases, the construction of our plans to feel safer requires application of several Asks. Our needs vary. What we need and how we express what we need, particularly from the Nine Asks, can change situationally. Many factors impact what makes us feel safe or threatened. The Asks that we need change depending on the environments where we dwell, the predicaments in which we find ourselves, the people with whom we are in fellowship, and our emotions in any given moment. We need more than just one Ask to traverse the rough terrain of human engagement; we need the Asks working together to feel safer, braver, and more courageous if we are to strive to be more genuine and authentic.

In shared spaces of all kinds, there is a continuum that exists in those who profess they want to do human being work better. At one end of the continuum, there are people who simply want to stop the complaining of those who live in identities that have been disenfranchised by the misuse of privilege and power. They may say things like, "Leave the past in the past." At the other end of the continuum are people deeply affected and troubled by their privileged identity and complicity, whether intended or not, with the misuse of privilege for a piece of power.

Folks who want to do and be better must know that change will not happen unless one emphatically cares about others. We can learn new, inclusive vocabulary. We can read and discuss case studies and scenarios to act out and practice wearing the lenses of others. We can share a carved-out moment to listen to speakers or share our own testimonials, regurgitating painful stories of oppressive spaces that negatively harmed and hurt us and others. But neither policies nor training procedures can make others care when they have made a conscious decision not to.

As hard as it is to accept, we are co-owners of the work of justice, inclusion, and belongingness, especially those who exhibit behaviors reflecting prejudice, power, and privilege. For several years, the corporate space used the term *ally* to demonstrate a person with access and authority who supports those with histories of disenfranchisement, marginalization, or oppression in some capacity. The challenge with this term is that a person in that role is not obligated to take any risks that will impact their safety and security. While allyship is appreciated, it is often a passive, noncommittal level of support—such as moderate effort to use the right language and display support in low-stakes situations. However, it takes much more than allyship to undo centuries of inequity and to right the wrongs of cultures and climates sustained by systemic bias. Most historically oppressed people, if forced to choose, would rather folks change behavior over language. Unlearning and acquiring new information has its place. Nevertheless, disenfranchised folks do not want to have a conversation about a book someone is reading if it does not result in their people being treated better and differently.

Instead of allyship, folks are now exploring the term *co-conspiratorship*. As a co-conspirator, historically oppressed people who share human spaces with you look for you to take risks. Much like their pursuit of justice, perpetual acceptance and belongingness is a risk. Pressing past allyship, co-conspiratorship asks you to make yourself vulnerable and ready to fight against the opposition, even if the opposition shares your identity lenses. The thought is that those with more freedom and agency have more safety and less to lose. A co-conspirator stands beside one whose identity has been historically threatened or oppressed, ready to risk their own safety and comfort. As a co-conspirator, you make yourself available to get dirty and to get in trouble—"good trouble," as the legendary John Lewis would say. How many people who are currently in a position of privilege and power are willing to give up access and comfort to suffer with people simply because they believe it is the right thing to do? Very few people choose to change continually on implicit, cognitive, and spiritual levels. And it's understandable; change is hard. Co-conspiratorship, unlike allyship, requires one to unlearn, relearn, and, most importantly, push back on oppressive practices to make traditional spaces that have felt threatening for others feel and be safer, braver, and more courageous.

Interesting things happen when one blends the theory of safer, braver, and more courageous spaces with the practice of yielding power. Few people desire to reflect on their own access, ability, and authority privileges deeply and introspectively. It's uncomfortable to believe one has been the cause of someone's suffering. Few are at ease facing the fact that their cherished grandparents or great grandparents may have implicitly (or explicitly) taught them to be biased toward or against certain groups of people. When unlearning-isms, biases, and prejudices, we must interrogate ourselves to grow and evolve. Growth is stifled, for example, when white folks argue with people of racialized non-white identities over the existence of white privilege. It is disheartening to hear men be dismissive of male privilege. It is threatening to experience heteronormative people be overtly dismissive or condemning of the existence and impact of homophobia and transphobia. It is one thing to be challenged by changing one's mindset. It is another thing if the challenge to change is received as a personal attack, and therefore, the new perspective is rejected and labeled a myth or a lie.

Application of the Nine Asks requires us to be introspective about who we are and how we show up in spaces that are shared with other human beings. It is imperative that we not only apply the Nine Asks to what we need from others in an any given space but also reflect on this safer space invitation and check ourselves on if we have any ways of being that interrupt the ability for safety to be practiced in its purest sense. Conversations, relationships, shared spaces, and just "doing life" with people requires us to be mindful of what we need from others and what others need from us.

There is personal introspection and application that must take place to embody the Nine Asks. We cannot ask others to be authentic if we are not showing up as our true selves. It is unfair of us to ask others to watch their words to protect our feelings but not be mindful of the power of our tongues. It would be disingenuous of us to be critical of others' judgmental stances while our thoughts are consumed with bias against others. How can we recognize better behavior if we are not exhibiting good behavior on our own? How can we be able to notice just treatment? Without our own practice, what would be the indicators of how justice felt? Our first example for any lesson in humanity should start with us as its students. It is incongruent to demand or even desire safer, braver, and more courageous spaces if we get (or remain) stuck in behavior patterns that are threatening, fearful, and cowardly.

When we engage with others, while holding the expectation that we will co-create and co-design an experience of safety, arguably the most egregious thing we can do is respond in a way that makes the experience hostile. In that example, we are at risk of abusing a trauma-informed environment and making it toxic. This happens more times than we care to admit.

You may really want to know, be, and do better as a human being. We can change, grow, and evolve; however, a singular conversation, event, or training session will *not* make you a different and altruistic person. When we make a commitment to change, it should be a lifelong pledge. It is a change in how we operate every day from the time we open our eyes until we fall back asleep in preparation for the next twenty-four hours. Change requires new behavior in every element of our lives. True application of the Nine Asks is reflected in how we show up in living, learning, and working spaces and even in our own minds, bodies, and spirits. If you change in one area of your life sincerely, the change has a higher likelihood of infiltrating every other space where we engage and interact with others. Real, sustaining change regarding human systems and relationships begins internally and flows outward.

The Nine Asks call for us to take better care of ourselves and simultaneously take into consideration the needs, well-being, and safety of others in a much wider, broader, and deeper way than our natural inclination typically permits. Reflect on experiences in your present-day neighborhoods and communities in comparison to stories and tales from those of our grandparents and their grandparents. We have much less interaction today with folks who live next door to us. We miss the sacredness of being Good Samaritans to our neighbors by instead adopting not-my-business attitudes, beliefs, and behaviors. The Nine Asks seek to make other folks' safety our business too. The Nine Asks urge us to explore the value of everyone's survival in each space, not just our own. They invite us to participate in a greater collective consciousness and to reflect on much deeper stories of safety. They require us to permeate some of the potentially uncomfortable nooks and crannies of our memories to have a better understanding of what makes us feel unsafe and why so that we can course correct our sometimes problematic and antiquated coping strategies. What if the only way to feel safer is by understanding why some core memories tell us we are less safe? What if the only way to feel braver is to insert ourselves into scenarios that make us feel afraid? What if the only way to be more courageous is to face fears where we have expressed and demonstrated cowardice in the past? The Nine Asks are hard to do because they ask us to operate in opposition of many of the survival instincts we have. Fear is a natural, hardwired emotion, and in fact, it may behoove us to lessen the frequency of advising folks to *not* be afraid. The Nine Asks challenge us to explore modification of behavior in the face of fear. They offer the approach of considering that fear is an expected companion on the journey along the human experience. The great news is that we *can* do hard things.

What does it look like to "do it" afraid? What is possible regarding the pursuit of human relationships if we explore connection while afraid? Fear has its place in protecting us from danger. But oftentimes, the perceived security gained from giving in to fear stunts our growth, limits our ability to evolve, and, in its worst-case scenario, regresses us from becoming the human beings we are fully capable of being. Through the ideal manifestation of the Nine Asks, we acknowledge fear *and* live emboldened lives with others and without confines. More realistically, a Nine Asks lifestyle is a prayer that we can outgrow fear and courageously tiptoe through the areas of unknown human engagement in search of light permeating darkness on the other side of our apprehensions.

Everyone wants to be well, but few want to take the "medicine" required to heal in our complicated and complex human existence. We drastically underestimate how many places and spaces do not feel safe — and that includes our own homes and our own families. Do we truly desire to see our growth edges improve? Are we honestly willing to sacrifice our own pride and discomfort to sustainably honor the humanity of others? Those who are leaders, guides, teachers, and active practitioners in creating safer human spaces have a heightened responsibility in how we create prospects for people to open up in conversation. Porous souls must not be left vulnerable, raw, and exposed with no plan on how to support them once their thoughts and behaviors begin shifting.

There are innumerable environments where we practice the human experience with others. Though we may not always be aware of how we exchange energy with others, we are always in the practice of human engagement, whether positive or negative. More times than not, our behaviors are unconscious. The next right thing for us to do is to be more intentional in *how* we share spaces. Think about how you present yourself for your employer and colleagues (or for your staff if you are the boss). Reflect on when you were a student in the classroom. What was school like for you? Does your house, apartment, or dwelling feel like home to you? The notion of safe spaces cannot be assumed. We must interrogate each atmosphere for the well-being of ourselves and others.

Our energy is contagious, both negatively and positively. When people notice our efforts to be better, they often level up and choose to explore who they are at their best as well. When we strive to evolve, we often do. What are you willing to do to be a better version of yourself—for yourself and for all the spaces in which you engage? The Nine Asks is not a check-the-box practice. It may challenge some of us to rewrite our origin stories. If practiced correctly, we should implicitly know who we are so that we can do a better job of understanding moments when shared space requires us to negotiate and have a little less of what we need to ensure someone else gets a little more of what they need. We all have value, beliefs, wants, and needs. Are you willing to modify or give up your wants and needs to demonstrate to someone else that you see them and care about what they need as well?

Declaring that a space is safe does not make it a safe space. Remember, safety is a person-specific concept based on their stories. What we can do is pursue measures to improve the conditions. We can reject the death sentence of perpetual discomfort. Numbing out in social spaces does not have to be our reality. Code-switching does not have to be the be-all and end-all to survive human systems. We can fight back against environments and people that seek to harm us as well as those that do not know better and hurt us. We can expect and demand that spaces be better hosts of human experiences. Interrogate yourself. Interrogate your ecosystem. Know that you are demonstrating some version of humanity everywhere you go, regardless of if your practices seek to honor or harm. You have the power to change the culture and climate in any environment. You have the power to help others practice being healthy, healed, and whole. Most of all, you have the right to receive exemplary treatment too. Safer spaces are for the greater good of all of us. It's time for us to do a progressive and more conscious job of making our wildest aspirational dreams of community in *every* space a reality.

CHAPTER 13

Practicing the Asks in Working Spaces

Whether your setting is a factory, cubicle farm, church office, fancy boardroom in the elusive "C-suite," or a classroom nestled in the ivory towers of higher education, going to work will, at some point, be an inevitability for most of us. It is assumed that gainfully employed folks show up for work, regardless of industry, as the most polished versions of themselves. We expect colleagues to attend business meetings as humans who are well accomplished, competent, capable, and confident about their skill sets and desired work objectives. What is sometimes missing in these spaces is individual and collective understandings and agreements on what each attendee needs to feel safer, braver, and more courageous. Work can be bigger than making widgets, though. We can endeavor to lean into the potential of holistic development within gainful employment (better known as the chaordic path first referenced in Ask #3). Within this prospect of possibility, leaders can produce a body of collective work bigger and better than what is accomplished individually. DEI, for example, should make the workplace stronger. But without felt safety in the office, humans struggle to maximize their potential.

If work feels unsafe, inquiries about colleagues' thoughts and ideas trigger memories, messages, and signals of a lack of safety. When these moments take place, impacted individuals leave their prefrontal cortexes and travel down to lower-level thinking. Threatened colleagues perform out of their amygdalae. Imagine brilliant thinkers sitting in a virtual meeting or in a conference room and instead of blowing the minds of their colleagues and ancestors, dysregulated professionals are trying to fix their faces, calm their tempers, monitor and censor their language, and prepare to cross-examine folks who they now perceive to be adversaries instead of allies, comrades, and co-conspirators for the greater good.

We would like to believe we always show up as experts and the best versions of ourselves, even when we are triggered in professional spaces. However, sometimes being petty wins. Sometimes tempers get the best of us. Sometimes flashes of emotions trigger those five *f*'s faster than logic and reasoning can arrive on the scene and rescue us from hypervigilance, dissociation, and bad decisions. The truth is that whether we choose to be or not, we show up in every space as whole people. We do not always respond well to tension and push-back. There are times when we have personal feelings in professional settings, and human responses or reactions are elicited. What happens when a negative work experience triggers familiar pain, discomfort, and distress? As whole people with complex brains that do not always segment memories as we desire, a challenging professional encounter may resurface past moments in our lives, be them personal or professional, when we felt unappreciated, unsafe, unprotected, and ultimately harmed.

Safety

How might we protect the integrity of our authentic selves and our whole beingness while at work? In other words, how do we understand and practice internal safety and felt safety in the workplace? There are likely endless amounts of strategies folks use. Some find and cling to their workplace besties. Some lean into hyper-fixation and get lost in their tasks. Others go silent and put themselves in a bubble. Still others treat work as an exclusively transactional experience. One of the most common strategies, though, is code-switching.

Somewhere, at some point, someone likely gave you challenging and arguably conflicting advice by encouraging you to keep your personal and professional lives separate. "Be who you need to be at work, and then be who you are (or want to be) at home." While the intent behind this guidance is understood, the fact of the matter is that we are whole people, and it is virtually impossible to truly sequester and section off aspects of identity and beingness to better enjoy the experience of living healthy, healed, and whole. We can attempt to behave as if we are fractions of a person in particular settings, but that might require us to deny aspects of who we are. For example, if you believe you are to separate your personal identity from your professional identity and only be the professional version of yourself at work, what would the expectation be for you to do with your feelings of physical sickness or pain while at work? What do you do with your worries over an ailing friend or family member? Should you be expected to *not* grieve over the loss of love or status or financial security because you are at work? Whether we display them or not, even when we are at work, our memories, feelings, emotions, fears, idiosyncrasies, predilections, values, opinions, and, yes, traumas have entered the workspace with us. We can and do give our best attempts at keeping our personal lives at bay; nevertheless, if our sensory receptors pick up any sight, scent, sound, touch, taste, or sixth sense that is adverse (whether we can consciously recall the memory or not), then logic, reasoning, creativity, and brilliance is out the window, and we will resort to survival-mode tactics.

Threats to Safety in Working Spaces

It has been said that where two or more are gathered, the Lord is there too. However, what we sense in some workspaces and meetings is not godly. The feeling that shows up appears to be a little more shadow than light. In places where the energy, vibe, and culture are a little heavier, there may be judgment and profound distrust. Depending on your industry, we are contracted to provide goods and services to clients, customers, and community for the purposes of fulfilling somebody's mission, vision, values, and objectives. Performance of assigned tasks may happen individually or with a team of others who have been hired based on their talents and skills interwoven with other skills on the team. At its best and at our best, we may be humbled by colleague accomplishments and grateful to be in the presence of minds who make it their business to ensure people are seen, heard, and appreciated. We may expect the work to inspire. Instead, what we frequently discover are feelings of uneasiness and anxiety, both with colleagues and leaders.

Bullying didn't stop on elementary school playgrounds, fear doesn't cease to exist once we leave home, and survival tactics are not exclusive to wilderness excursions. The moment we feel unappreciated or devalued at work, safety has been threatened and our prefrontal cortexes immediately go offline. In these instances, we may feel an overwhelming need to protect ourselves. This protection might be displayed in a myriad of ways, including assertively defending our ideas or weaponizing silence to form a protective boundary. Coworkers are often othered and excluded for all kinds of reasons, such as for their thoughts, ideas, or expressions. When we better understand how trauma shows up in our bodies, we can recognize one of the first signs of the shifting from our prefrontal cortexes to our amygdalae. When we feel unsafe, our bodies respond—even at work. You might feel strain, tension, and dis-ease as if you are being restricted from movement or carrying weight that is heavier than you can bear. There might be pressure or tightness in your head, shoulders, neck, or back. Perhaps your gut is triggered by stress at work, and you suddenly need to use the restroom. Exhaustion and fatigue go to work with us. Scan your body when you feel your value and worth are in question at work. What do you notice?

Working spaces can start with a room full of leaders who are demonstratively successful by their own merit. Suddenly, a threat emerges, and these same successful souls are faced with slower progress, foggy forecasts, and a need to ask for help—if courageous enough to do so. These can be uncharted waters. In so many other areas of our lives, we have all the answers. We are the go-tos. We make things happen. We have track records of victories and achievements. It is likely some of us have been forced to lead in other areas of our lives based on necessity as opposed to having the power to choose. It is hard to turn off *all* those experiences and to exist in opposition to our learned behavior and rename the opposition "growing" or "stretching." Realistically, growth may feel like challenge and can stir emotions of anger and fear. Where there is fear, close behind is the threat and overwhelming compulsion to defend against and survive the threat: the threat to one's name and legacy; the threat of how we always do it; the threat to an old idea; the threat of change; the threat of undoing culture, regardless of if the existing culture is toxic or not. We are beautiful, powerful, brilliant humans who have so much resting on our shoulders, and the truth is that we do not always know what to do. The unknown is scary for any human being, especially leaders, and our reactions to fear are human. Grace abounds.

Many of us have struggle and survival stories that are not disclosed in corporate and market spaces. That means the right to collectively access historical context as to why we are so tough, so rigid, so committed, and so passionate about our perspectives is not automatically given or earned. We see the what in the space, but we do not know the why behind the posturing and behaviors of others. Knowing the why can make all the difference in us being a little more patient and understanding with someone we perceive to be difficult. Understanding transforms an adversary and a difficult person into a complex human being worthy of compassion. There is a difference, and within that difference is the opportunity to gift more safety and courage to us and others.

When Asks Go Wrong: Worst Behavior at Work

What happens when the lack of a safer, braver, and more courageous space persists? When you are not at your best, the work may technically get done, but in your honest opinion, is it your best individual and collective work? Good ideas may surface; however, greatness may not be birthed if most parties involved are in survival mode. When we do not trust the space or each other, it shows up in what we produce and how we serve. When we are not at our best, we have the propensity to feel threatened by inquiries and questions. Curiosity can feel accusatory and like doubt. When colleagues feel invisible, diminished, or taken for granted in the space, that stirs up the five *f*'s: fight, flight, freeze, fawn, and flock. When fear, discomfort, anxiety, and anger win, the moral imperative behind the work suffers.

What happens if you believe in your capability to do good work, but you have a felt sense that you and your cerebral prowess are not validated? Imagine being an expert but treated as a novice, knowing yourself to be a leader but supervised like a widget worker, or offering suggestions for solutions but handled and managed as if you were the problem. Toxic workspaces can create narratives that typecast employees as incompetent. Misunderstood workers are sometimes portrayed as lacking readiness or ability to do assigned work. In these instances, rebuff arguments that paint people as problems in circumstances when the environment is to blame. Consider extending healthy inquiry to the folks who create or sustain threatening workplace culture. We must do all we can to ensure that we and the spaces that employ us are not barriers to people's gifts and anointing.

Thrown to the Wolves: Mallory's Story

County officials launched a special program in response to BIPOC complaints about discriminatory practices at the local business center. The pilot program's intent was to provide job opportunities for previously denied and disenfranchised community members. The initiative was met with mixed reviews, and very few citizens were satisfied with its execution. Mallory was hired two years later as an expert to audit the effectiveness of the program and conduct research for improvement recommendations. The consultant assembled a team of subject-matter experts and designed a plan to meet with community members from various constituency groups for feedback. Her research tour attracted a great deal of criticism and controversy due to race, class, and political biases regarding the program's mission, objectives, and, most especially, its BIPOC benefactors. In the last phase of the audit, the core team prepared for a final gathering with the most vocal dissenters of the program.

Mallory and her four-member core team arrived an hour early to set up the room. Previous events hosted an average of six to eight people, but this session attracted twenty RSVPs, most of whom were older, successful professionals and business owners. Following protocol of prior community forums, Birdie, the team's dialogue facilitator, welcomed everyone to the event and introduced Mallory to kick off the gathering. Mallory began sharing details on the auditing process, status, and next steps. This five-minute update lasted for nearly an hour due to threatening, dangerous, and unsafe diatribe from the crowd directed at the core team; and Mallory was the lightning rod for their malice. The team knew of the constituency group's exasperation with the program and auditing process as they had vocalized numerous complaints. County officials' responses to BIPOC charges of discrimination were perceived by the constituency group of the evening as counter-discriminatory, and they believed themselves to be victims of injustice with rights to special opportunities as well. Contrary to the intended purpose of the night's conversation, the audience used the gathering and Mallory's power-adjacent position to vehemently attack her, the program, and elected officials they deemed responsible for their displeasure. The audience was volatile, screaming, yelling, and, in some instances, pointing and cursing at Mallory as she attempted to respond to their questions and demands.

The behavior of the attendees was unparallel to any other program event to date. The core team was stunned with emotional responses spanning the five *f*'s (fight, flight, freeze, fawn, and flock). Birdie, who'd experienced workplace trauma in her past, breathed deeply to slow her shift into a fighting survival tactic. She interrupted Mallory and spoke directly to the audience with sternness, frustration, and disapproval. She declared in an authoritative voice that their outbursts were unwarranted, offensive, and misguided. Birdie de-escalated the attacks, refocused the conversation on the assigned topic, and reminded participants that Mallory was not their real target. A leader from within the constituency group encouraged the attendees to calm down and listen to what the meeting hosts had to say. Mallory stepped back in to continue her responses to questions. Within minutes, the room again escalated with even more passion, fervor, and fire than before. Now instead of attacks coming from a select few, the loud voices, conflict, and disruption erupted throughout the room. Some turned their attention, angst, and fury to Birdie following her interruption. Moments from completely shutting down and walking out of the space, the facilitator interrupted the dissension a second time and silenced the participants. She gathered her composure, astonished at the visceral emotions of the room, and explained that attendees were responding from a place of fear and anger, which clouded their intended message and greater sentiments.

Mallory remained in the front of the room, disrespected and stupefied at what had just taken place. Rowan, the project manager, and Gemma, the documentarian, observed with flushed cheeks, accelerated heart rates, and wide eyes. There were no constructive thoughts or helpful inquiries contributed. Instead of reflective thinking, participants had pounced on Mallory. Allocated time for the targeted dialogue was now compromised; Birdie was at risk of not accomplishing the task at hand due to repeated disruption and dysregulation of the space. She, again, expressed despondence in their treatment of Mallory. The constituency group representative stood and pleaded for restraint from attendees. Silence fell on the room.

Some looked relieved at Birdie's re-grounding of the momentum. Others looked angered and insulted at her audacious attempt to command the room. Nevertheless, she moved forward and, with the help of her colleagues, facilitated the conversation as designed and in accordance with the other sessions. Mallory, Rowan, and Gemma captured meticulous notes, and at the end of the event, Birdie was careful to extend cordial thanks to attendees for their time, thoughts, and feedback. The team then began packing up supplies and clearing the room.

Prior to exiting, select community members pulled core team members to the side and shared additional, thinly veiled political thoughts, opinions, and viewpoints about the program. Some commentary was even bigoted and factually incorrect. The team listened to audience members without response as they filed out the room one by one. Once the space was vacant, Mallory, Gemma, Rowan, and Birdie decompressed in informal dialogue for an hour about the unexpected and unprecedented volatile nature of the meeting. It took weeks for the four team members to recover mentally from the event.

Safer Working Space: Reflection and Considerations

On rare occasions, it takes something greater than talent and tenacity to survive the job. The aforementioned team's experiences—especially Mallory's and Birdie's—are cautionary tales of what goes wrong when we do not ground workplace relationships in the Nine Asks. Before, during, and after their unfortunate experience, the core team members needed to feel safe, but the meeting felt untrustworthy and changed the work dynamics in a way that made them feel unsettled.

Be cautious and interrogate how terminology like *safe* and *unsettled* is utilized. It would be easy for one to believe that the anxiety or apprehension in a circle of colleagues is because of terms like *inadequacy, imposter syndrome,* or *insecurity.* Mallory, for example, was exceptionally qualified for her role, but she was treated as if she was clueless and powerless. While these conditions, experiences, and perspectives do have their place, they are not always the reason why folks struggle to perform, excel, and succeed in the workplace. In many instances, people can have complete confidence in their talents, gifts, and abilities. They know their areas of strength and excellence just as many other grown and experienced folks do. That said, there is a difference between not trusting oneself and feeling a perceived (or real) lack of safety at work, which can compromise professional trust and subsequently negatively impact workplace performance. There was no trust between the meeting attendees and the core team. Subsequently, no one felt safe.

In the chapter on Ask #1, we explained how the brain processes stress and trauma. Using the case of Thrown to the Wolves, it is probable that most of the humans in the room operated from their amygdalae once anger or fear set in. The amygdala's primary focus is survival. Coarse conversation, argumentativeness, avoidance, and other strong behavioral responses reflected emotions of folks engaging in lower-level thinking, which utilizes very little logic, reasoning, and executive functioning.

At our best, when we feel safe, brave, and courageous, we can execute our most superior thinking. We are creative and innovative because there is no distraction externally or internally from our highest level of thinking. However, when unwanted interruptions, such as sleep deprivation, hunger, pain, grief, heartache, stress, or a myriad of other symptoms, make cameo appearances in our bodies, our amygdalae come to life. We can't always control how our brains try to take care of us, and we certainly can't put physiological manifestations of distress on a timer to complete their cycles of mayhem before our shifts in the office begin. When there is the implicit, subconscious, and, in some cases, supernatural predilection that we are in danger or are threatened in any way, our natural neurological design signals the amygdala to take over and foster our survival of the moment or experience. More clearly and directly stated, if your brain must choose between being brilliant or surviving, it will invariably choose to survive first—even when you're in an important meeting or attending a conference. When we are charged to do our best thinking to problem-solve a challenging situation but we do not feel safe or comfortable, we will struggle to show up and perform at our best.

Another important consideration regarding trauma, safer spaces, and work involves memory. The hippocampus connects sensations and emotions to memories. Have you ever received a negative trigger, such as a smell, taste, touch, or auditory signal, and were reminded of something traumatic that you had to fight to survive? You have your hippocampus to thank for that. Your sensory receptors can receive a signal and create a physiological reaction that causes your body to remember something your mind forgot. For example, a specific kind of sub was served for refreshments at Mallory's trainwreck town hall meeting. It is possible that the sight or smell of those subs years from now could recall the intensity of perceived and real threat Mallory experienced in that event. This might explain moments when we are being productive, and we lose our mojo. Dysregulation (the inability to control our emotional responses) distracts us from producing our best work during a task. Essentially, while we are being efficient and effective, triggers tell our brains that all its resources are needed to survive something as opposed to create or innovate a new concept or idea. The memories we hold on to and store become more real than the present moment. We react based on the memory and become anxious. Past experiences predict future consequences.

Our brains operate like supercomputers, constantly pushing information through different channels to aid in functioning through every moment and experience. Note that this process is not overtly positive or negative; it just *is*. The overall processes, though, can continuously inform and update how we perceive safety and threat at work. Once we understand how our brains operate and process information, it gives us ample opportunity to grace ourselves when we don't react as desired in any given situation. We are still, in spirit, young versions of ourselves who seek the same needs to be seen, heard, felt, and appreciated as we did when we were children. Those needs never go away. The desire to be safe and affirmed never disappears and is a fair request in any environment, including and especially at work. We develop coping strategies along the journey of life to respond to our safety needs, and those practices follow us in all scenarios, regardless of the setting. As we get older and hopefully wiser, we may come to discover that measures we used to protect ourselves when we were younger are not always as productive, beneficial, or functional when we are older. We often commit to extreme protective measures to feel safe when the holistic work of healing lies in aligning resources on mental, spiritual, and emotional levels.

When Asks Are Well Practiced

Healthy employment should not require us to regulate ourselves and do inner-child work to better understand root causes for feeling triggered in meetings. We can seek clarity on what goes wrong in the workspace and what we all can do to make things right, meaning safer, braver, and more courageous. With centering from our higher power *plus* our prefrontal cortexes (back) online, we can experience regulation at work. With a deeper understanding of the people and situations at play, we can give and receive more clarity, grace, and patience in occupational settings. Consider how applying the Nine Asks could help create a safer and braver space for challenging professional situations:

—*Aąk #1, Be aą Honeąt and Vulnerable aą Poąąible.* Make sure anger is not the engine powering the honesty. Anger is often a secondary emotion. Its close relative, rage, is guaranteed to end with detonating the five *f*'s. Try waiting until you are grounded and regulated before engaging in dialogue with others, especially in the workplace.

—*Aąk #2, Reąpect Boundarieą and Threąholdą.* It's far easier to overstep others' boundaries when you feel as if yours have been violated. Similarly, if you are at or have exceeded your maximum capacity, it will be much harder to gauge and adhere to someone else's thresholds for pain and discomfort. If you are at work and concerned about how much you can take or how long you can last before losing your cool, consider grounding yourself and then grounding others. If, by chance, the grounding doesn't work, consider rescheduling the meeting or event. It is better to delay the work than to deny ourselves healthy work relationships.

—*Aąk #3, Practice No Judgment.* We are not always able to prove unequivocally that bias is to blame when there is tension in the workplace. However, microaggressions or thinly veiled insults are typical forms of workplace judgment. Be in constant practice of your self-care activities to stay calm and remain open. Porous minds deliver better work.

—*Aąk #4, Honor Confidentiality.* We are extensions of our workplace performances for sure. But we are also whole people with whole narratives that cannot be encompassed exclusively through the lens of who we are on the job. We have a right to own, tell, and defend our stories—or not—even on the clock.

—*Aąk #5, Come Back to Me.* Workplace communication, especially with leadership, may be imbalanced. Some get tons of talk time while others never make a sound or demand attention. Notice when you take up too much space. Interrogate yourself if you consistently seek (or benefit from) the spotlight, while others never seem to speak. You're likely not making enough room for others to shine. Particularly when emotions are high, give folks time and ways to process before contributing to the workspace. Always circle back and let people know their presence is worthy of a check-in and their voice has sustainable value that deserves to be highlighted.

—*Ask #6, Respect the Process of Learning the "Right" Language.* Ego is often to blame for all the ways this Ask results in loud and wrong behavior or a closed mouth that doesn't get fed. Be (or stay) open to new, revised, and corrected ways of thinking. We must hold each other accountable to speak up and share so that we can all learn from others' perspectives. Make a practice of thanking others when they teach you something new.

—*Ask #7, Take the Time to Listen First.* Be cautious about when your internal dialogue starts planning a response before the speaker is done talking. You might know the answer to their question. You might have a smart quip to reply to something they said. But are you certain about what is being asked of you as a listener in that moment? Folks have a right to engage in communication that is not one-sided. Dialogue is about flow. We listen to learn, and we talk when a response is needed. There's power in compassionate silence and in correctly reacting to the speaker's requests.

—*Ask #8, Grant Permission to Go Deeper or Decline.* This is one of the optimal ways to exercise healthy curiosity about the people, places, and things linked to your profession. In addition to increased knowledge about mission-driven deliverables, asking is the only route to learning more about the people you spend at least half your day with. That said, the intent of work is usually not personal. So, if your human inquiries get declined, remember that colleagues are well within their rights to deny your request to get personal (or to wait for a coffee or lunch break to pull you to the side and share a little more).

—*Ask #9, Stay in Your Seat.* Being present might also involve getting out of your own head. There is a high likelihood we don't give work consistent, unbroken, and undivided attention for forty-plus hours per week. Some of that time gets wasted in moments when we're checked out. Whether it's your body, mind, or spirit getting in the way, try to satisfy your physiological needs early so that you can stay present when it matters most. Don't let lack of focus or dysregulation highjack your professionalism. Keep up with your self-care homework so that you can be present, on task, and on point when you're on the clock.

The Nine Asks allow us to share our honest perspective about where we feel vulnerable and uncomfortable with existing culture (Ask #1). We can pay better attention to the rising signs and signals about our boundaries and thresholds (Ask #2). We can be more aware of the judgment present in spaces we encounter by separating facts from opinions and values (Ask #3). With more trust, perhaps we can believe in the Ask for confidentiality so that we can own how our stories are told and shared (Ask #4). Some colleagues lack voice, fail to access power in speaking up, and struggle to be heard. We can come back to them in meetings with sustained welcoming behavior and ongoing invitations for them to share their voices and perspectives (Ask #5). When we are not in alignment about communication, language, and expression, we can demonstrate more patience with one another about the process of understanding what words mean and that both words and approach matter (Ask #6). When we are in defense of our own intellect, ideas, and integrity, we do not do the best job of taking the time to listen first (Ask #7). At our best, we can listen wholly and intently instead of preparing counterarguments when the chaordic path emerges. In moments when we feel challenged, prickled, or even threatened, increased safety allows us permission to be curious about others' expressed ideas and concerns (Ask #8). Finally, there are some who shut down in moments where a break in focus turns into absolute power failure. Survival mode is exhausting and prevents folks from staying connected, involved, and engaged. However, a culture that includes regulation (or practices to manage extreme emotions, sensations, and thoughts) can give us the energy to stay in our seats, even when work is heavy and hard (Ask #9).

CHAPTER 14

Practicing the Asks in Learning Spaces

In consideration of learning spaces, it helps to reflect on the chaordic path. On one extreme of the continuum, there is chaos. When we are overwhelmed or have too much distraction and overstimulation, the distraction creates too much noise around us, causing dysregulation, which negatively impacts growth and learning. Unrestricted chaos can turn into mayhem. On the opposite end of the chaordic path continuum is order. Order can sometimes stifle creativity and autonomy. When we are bored or have too much order imposed on us, the situation is at risk of transforming into imposition and control. When we are controlled and disempowered, we do not grow.

Our greatest opportunity to level up exists in the middle; we thrive in the tension between chaos and order. All our best learning, growing, and thinking happens when we are a little uncomfortable and challenged. This is the sweet spot. Very rarely do we challenge ourselves to get to this place. Most of the time, if given the choice, we opt to be and stay comfortable. Human beings make our decisions based on whichever choice is the *least* painful. We can stay in a seemingly insurmountable volume of chaos, confusion, disorganization, dysfunction, and disorder as long as it does not require us to have to change anything. We also have infinite examples of feeling disempowered, smothered, isolated, voiceless, and downright invisible. Yet, we do not challenge or force our way out of shadows into light. Instead, we allow our eyes to get adjusted to the gloom, and in extreme cases, we rebrand it as a skill set.

Sometimes adults refer to these conditions as "the devil we do know versus the devil we don't know." We may say to ourselves, "My job is awful, but at least I'm employed." "I'm already miserable in the relationship." All roads point to the same concluding rhetorical question: If I already know what to expect, why change? How do we become complacent? When we are young, the experience of being stuck is intolerable. Before we are taught that change and challenge is negative, we are excited to learn new things. Who among us has not felt the agitation of a child trying our patience when they attempt to teach themselves how to tie their own shoes? Or whistle? Or snap? Or blow a balloon? The anticipation of successfully completing a new and unprecedented challenge can keep a focused child busy for an absurd amount of time. As we get older, the first sight of stretch, challenge, struggle, or growth edges can cause us to drop everything and run back to what we know.

So, whether we are working with youth in a school or another educational environment or entering a space as a learner ourselves, let us ask: When opportunities present themselves for us to stretch and grow, can and will we choose to keep ourselves in a space of discomfort to become better versions of ourselves? Will we seek safety, bravery, and courage in moments when we need them most? Have teachers and educators—across all levels as well as in traditional and nontraditional capacities—prepared their class-rooms, training rooms, and other knowledge-transference spaces to be culturally affirming and aesthetically rich environments that allow learners to feel comfortable enough to be (and stay) in their frontal cortexes?

In the following sections, a young adult storyteller and a youth storyteller share lived experiences where learning spaces fell short of being safer, braver, and more courageous. Through their chronicles, try to glean examples of what happens when teaching and learning take place on opposite ends of the chaordic path. Consider these scenarios and the danger of a learning space having too little structure or too much structure. In both instances, the extremes get in the way of students reaching their greatness. The balance of the chaordic path, including and especially in learning spaces, provides a climate for people to feel safer, braver, and courageous enough to grow.

Not Enough and Too Much: Threats to Safety in Learning Spaces

Youth, young adulthood, and K-12 education environments are difficult for virtually everyone. They are awkward. Puberty wreaks havoc on students' appearance, hygiene, thoughts, and feelings. They don't quite have the gait of their walk figured out. One of the most frustrating things about being in middle school or watching middle schoolers is students may appear grown-*ish*, and even when they are maturing, they are still what some affectionately and culturally refer to as "babies." They do not yet know who they are, and in many cases, they are emulating the identities of other people they see, who they assume have things figured out. The secret they will discover later is their young idols do not know who they are either. Prepubescence and puberty are, in general, a hot mess of confusion and misfit identity.

Though youth with whom we have relationships may share a vast majority of our values, humor, culture, and affinities, one thing we may not share from generation to generation is the social norms of our peers during the primary years. Young students, especially those with risky behavior patterns, are drinking and misusing drugs early. They are sexually active earlier too. Students are harming themselves and contemplating suicide at higher rates than ever before. Because we are afraid of controversial topics and conversations, we lie to ourselves and say youth are not ready to speak on such topics. In truth, they have been waiting for us to see them and honor their young, forming humanity for years.

Consider the race and ethnicity of your household, neighborhoods, and schools while you were growing up in comparison to youth you know in your family or community now. Factor into the equation religion, neurodiversity, mental health, gender identity and expression, sexual orientation, class, socioeconomic status, and upward mobility. School is different today than it was just a couple decades ago. As such, the concept of safety is ever-changing. However, some elements of danger and threat have not changed. There is not enough research, evidence, documentaries, or story formats to accurately share the true lived experience of Black and Brown people, particularly in predominantly white spaces and especially in kindergarten through high school. For many youths, the higher the socioeconomic status climbs, the more bizarre the social experience gets for all young people involved, including and especially othered young people. Lottie, a Black, female college student, explains her suburban elementary and middle school years as, "seven years of bad experiences with friends." Her story was replete with awkward school days, and the residue of discomfort followed her into her collegiate learning spaces.

Not Enough Safety: Lottie's Story

Middle school years were a blur of emotional pain and peer pressure for Lottie. Bullying was disguised as playful friendships, and she was made to feel miserable about her intellect, body, hair, and race for several years. Due to the impact of bullying, by her freshman year of high school, she was, in many ways, broken and fractured. She had low self-esteem and a poor grasp of self-efficacy. During this formidable academic season in her life, it may be significant to note that her guardians were employed as executive leaders in similar unsafe workspaces. Adults, especially BIPOC adults, know disenfranchised students struggle to find a place in an environment that, on at least an implicit level, communicates that they are not wanted. BIPOC working guardians battle people, places, and things designed to disempower, and they are then charged to serve and support students who are minimalized and made to feel invisible all day, especially through the lens of race. Parents of othered students, especially parents who do not have identities categorized as lenses within the power majority, regularly experience discomfort at work while their children experience discomfort at school. And when parent and child can finally retreat to home base, vicarious trauma results in them spending nights and weekends rebuilding themselves and each other so that they will be strong enough to go back to work and school and risk the high likelihood of being torn down by unsafe spaces all over again.

Lottie faced several microaggressive issues inside and outside the classroom with her peers as well as her teachers. However, she felt conflicted asking for help from her culturally conscious yet overprotective parents. Outspoken advocacy and activism (e.g., "I'm coming up to the school!") did not make her feel safe as it brought additional unwanted attention her way. One can have the most profoundly polished professional demeanor and a formal education to back up said posture of being an intellectual person. However, if a person who serves as a protector of children believes a child is being harmed in any way, it is very easy to drop the formalities and become both crass and confrontational to demand and defend the safety and protection of one's precious person. Is this the best response? Is there a more effective way for parents, guardians, advisors, behavioral wellness professionals, and educators to support, encourage, and advocate for safer spaces in schools?

Lottie often returned home from school feeling dejected and hurt. Her guardians usually had more questions than answers or advice, which did not make Lottie feel supported emotionally in the moment. Where were the adults? Lottie felt vulnerable, unsafe, profoundly uncomfortable, and completely unprotected in school. How do teachers miss racist commentary from white students to Black students in classrooms and hallways? How do staff members not notice the absence of Black and Brown students involved in extracurricular social activities? How is it possible to have even a small but present critical mass of underrepresented students but not have resources and support systems to affirm their identities inside the school building? Does anyone notice them? Is anyone protecting them? The more difficult question is does anyone even acknowledge that students in racialized Black and Brown bodies or students in any disenfranchised identity for that matter might need protection on a more holistic level?

Perhaps the most egregious is when teachers are complicit in the harm of students. In Lottie's words,

"Part of what made me feel super uncomfortable when I was in school, [was] not only that the teachers didn't believe when things would happen, but actually most of what made me uncomfortable was my teachers partaking in the making fun of people and the gossip. Like Ms. P constantly ripping on me. I can look back on certain memories and I realize I spent all my high school years thinking that some of my favorite teachers liked me, and they clearly did not. I ate on the risers and [my favorite] teacher screamed at me and made me cry. That's not normal for your favorite high school teacher. Or Mr. H choosing Veronica to be the editor-in-chief for the yearbook because he liked gossiping with her. My seventh-grade orchestra teacher constantly made weird kinds of racially charged comments towards the Black students. He would always make weird jokes about our lips and not like in a sexual way but in a racial way. I remember thinking that made me so uncomfortable. It made me never want to go to class. Like if I really didn't care back then, y'all think I would have been up in that class? There's no way. There's no way. I would never go back and subject myself to that. Not for all the money in the world."

From her sophomore year of high school through her collegiate experience, Lottie suffered moment after moment where teachers and educators from various positions within the educational system missed the mark and the call to serve as protectors for students. In some cases, teachers were as malicious and nasty as the young people who sat in their classrooms. Lottie recalled many instances when teachers engaged in gossip, chatter, and instigation regarding students' personal lives. The young people didn't have the opportunity to experience Ask #4 and to be their own storytellers. When we don't control our stories, we lose the ability to have power over our realities. She shared stories of teachers whose students trusted them with sensitive matters, and the teachers did not believe them. Students needed help, support, and wise counsel from the adults around them. Unfortunately, they were disappointed by adults not believing that an issue was serious enough to investigate. She rarely saw microaggressive behaviors met with consequences and repercussions for behaviors that harmed students. The alternative she experienced was adults who didn't believe an issue existed at all. She witnessed adults who knew of potential harm for students, and instead of protecting the students, they either protected themselves or other adults or turned a blind eye to the source of the threat.

Ask DEI professionals across all industries; they have seen and heard surreal and unbelievable stories. Both students and educators have given firsthand accounts of instances when teachers engaged in inappropriate sexual relationships with young people. It is not unheard of for teachers to call out students because of their names or to manage student relationships in ways that align with stereotype threat. There is empirical research that demonstrates evidence of tracking students into more and less advanced classes, providing white students opportunities and the benefit of the doubt to prove their intellect and potential to handle difficult coursework. While on the other hand, low-income and BIPOC students were tracked to lower-level courses because it was believed, whether explicitly or implicitly, that they were doing said students a favor and not forcing them to do work they were perceived to not be academically prepared to do. There is an old saying, "The road to hell is paved with good intentions." How does expecting less from a student communicate care? These are just a few examples of nightmares and worst-case scenarios that occur inside of learning communities where students are not provided with the environments needed to be the best versions of themselves. Although it is a tough question to ask, we must interrogate ourselves on if we, as adults, are the best versions of ourselves when there are young people in our care.

It cannot be understated that the traumas we experience, especially as children, are not our fault. However, it is our responsibility to pursue our healing. Lottie experienced tremendous emotional hardships throughout her schooling that made it difficult for her to believe she could be successful. It was a fight to get her through high school. When it was time to apply for college, Lottie hesitated because she didn't believe that she was mentally strong enough to handle a more rigorous educational setting. Willing herself to pursue the possibility of change, in the eleventh hour, she applied for admittance into colleges and ended up attending a midwestern, predominantly white institution. Even in higher education, as one of the only Black students in her creative writing major, she experienced microaggressions discomforting enough to make her withdraw from the major and change her focus of study. Not only that, but the pressure of being an atypical Black girl impaired her felt safety in social settings on campus. The dissonance of not being Black enough for Black people but being too Black in predominantly white spaces proved to be overwhelming. After the completion of her sophomore year as a virtual student during the epidemic of COVID, Lottie chose the pursuit of her holistic wellness as a priority and sat out for a gap year of self-care.

Upon her return to college, she reflected on what she would need to show up in her classrooms and workspaces feeling safe enough to be her true self. Two words stood out in her asks: empathy and accountability. These virtues are two of many expected outcomes from the Nine Asks, particularly Ask #2, Respect Boundaries and Thresholds; Ask #4, Honor Confidentiality; and Ask #7, Take the Time to Listen First. To win the war against perceived threats internally and externally, we must demonstrate empathy. Whether we were discussing her peer circles or the adults in her life who attempted to be support systems, Lottie needs to believe that people have a willingness to truly see her and accept her in her fullness. She understands the complexities of her personality as well as her battles to fight through anxiety and depression daily. We must be compassionate about meeting someone where they are and hold space with them and for them, even when we do not know what to say or how to be. Even when we cannot provide exactly what a person needs, we can be open and present.

As to her second ask, for accountability, when we drop the ball — and we will from time to time — we must ask ourselves what are we willing to do to make things better? The explication of the Nine Asks in part 2 included roadblocks as well as tips for execution (and repair) when creating safe spaces gets tough. How can we right our wrongs? What efforts should we put into practice to repair the ruptures when the breaks in trust happen? How do we ensure that a fracture in a relationship becomes Japanese kintsugi art instead of a fault line ready to tremble and collapse the entire relationship? For young people to feel safer in our learning spaces, we must show up for them holistically. This requires us to hold ourselves and one another accountable when we get it wrong. Accountability is part of the process on the journey toward making things right.

We wait too late to talk to young people about risky behavior, safety practices, and holistic wellness; we should start conversations with older elementary school students. On grade school and middle school playgrounds, youth hold conversations about abortion, religion, undocumented immigrants, and viewpoints on skin color, race mixing, and multinational identity. Very adult topics find their way by swing sets and sliding boards. How did taboo topics such as politics and religion melt into the palettes of the mouths of young people with baby teeth and popsicle stains on their faces? Adults drastically underestimate the range of conversational content shared in the presence of children that shape their opinions early on and impede their ability to love without bias. How many of the Nine Asks are violated in youth social spaces before we are practiced in the art of socialization? When is the right time to teach human engagement to young people before it's too late?

Our "new normal," including social media, school shootings, pandemics, mental illness crises, and unprecedented events in recent history, has forced caregivers to rethink how we approach, engage, support, and protect young people. Kids these days are different and rightfully so. Teenagers of a certain age, particularly those born after 2005 have no memory of social media not existing. They have access to the entire world with a login and a swipe. Whether it's on the news, in their digital messages, or on the timelines of the platforms where they socialize, it is virtually impossible for us to shield children, particularly those who experience othering based on their identities, from seeing folks—who look like most of their teachers and school administrators—discriminate against and even "unalive" people who look like their family members. They have watched the persecution, torture, and assassination of Black folks, trans community members, non-Christian aunties and uncles, and other faces of people who look familiar and have names that sound like kin. Boomers and Gen Xers have no concept of what it's like to be a pubescent child with multimedia access to the world via wireless computers in your phone, effortlessly see death on said devices that fit in your pockets, and then log out of the virtual world to do algebra homework. It must take a certain level of dissociation to see endless news reels of violence and then swipe to transition to a music-streaming platform. This is the new normal for our young people. We expect greatness out of them all while they struggle to attain basic psychological safety. Some do not expect to live long enough to meet our expectations.

Too Much Control: Grae's Story

Grae felt disconnected from and misunderstood by the adults in her life. They claimed to care for her and wanted to support her, but they often seemed closed off and punitive in their engagement with her, especially when she was in crisis. Her discomfort came to a head after January 6, 2021. So many unknowns had taken place in the world between January 2020 and January 2021; now this. Grae logged on for school following the unprecedented US Capitol insurrection, feeling wholly unsafe and ungrounded and fearing the end of the world was near. Students were advised to trust and seek adults, such as parents, educators, coaches, and other caregivers for support. However, for Grae and her peers, seeking adult support was exceedingly stressful. Their contact points either didn't have answers to hard questions or simply would not engage in deeper dialogue. What youth didn't know is that the adults could not effectively relate with what it was like for Grae and her peers during a moment in history that included a global pandemic, a bias-filled presidential election, and then a Capitol insurrection. Grae felt very afraid; and with no one around to give her advice, the fear grew. She reached out to people she looked up to, put her faith in, and took hold of to gauge if they could help make sense of things. They had nothing of benefit to share with her, often redirecting her to focus on school or stay off social media. She realized the adults around her were not comfortable talking about the state of the world. While good intentions were hopefully at the center of these behaviors, the adults around her were avoiding discussion about serious matters. In trying to prevent youth from feeling more worried and anxious, the avoidance of conversation backfired.

As unprecedented local, national, and world events continued to unfurl, it made Grae's paranoia only worse. It was as if the world was about to be wiped out. People were dying, and it seemed as if no one cared. When she attempted to have honest discussions with teachers and support staff, educators did not respond in a way that was open, curious, or comforting. They silenced the inquiries and redirected students back to class. Grae wondered if their responses were an effort to escape from fear themselves. She had never experienced anything like what she was witnessing in the news and suspected it was difficult to cope for everyone. She yearned to talk about really terrifying experiences.

Dissociation and social-emotional shutdown are one of the many concerning consequences when young people are exposed to man's inhumanity to man and then struggle to live and learn in places that are not open to discussing these kinds of events. Grae barely passed sixth grade and narrowly escaped repeating seventh grade. Her chores were routinely incomplete; she slept all the time and had dropped out of long-standing extracurricular activities. All she seemed to do was sit in her room and video chat with friends. Grae's parents were exhausted with her total disengagement at home and school. Their initial reaction to her perceived insubordination was restriction and consequence. Punishment seemed like the appropriate, familiar response. But Grae's issues weren't old school issues; hers were new, unprecedented problems.

Once COVID quarantining ended the ability for young people (and really everyone) to socialize with each other, it was the proverbial nail in the coffin. Just as masks went up and doors closed, youth serotonin levels plummeted. School wasn't safe. Home wasn't safe. The world no longer felt safe. Grae as well as other young people assumed the unrequested responsibility of being pseudo-therapists to everyone on their texting threads, not trusting adults with their heaviness. When in-person interaction was deemed all but illegal during COVID, their only ability to connect with one another was through their smart devices. Phones were not necessarily barriers to their success, safety, and well-being. On the contrary, sometimes cell phones and social media were lifelines to coping strategies, stories that validated feelings, and other unexpected mental wellness resources.

Imagine being a young student besieged with an unprecedented reality of performing online course assignments, receiving instruction through videoconferencing technology, and feeling incredibly dysregulated but being threatened with disciplinary actions if you do not "turn on your video cameras." Could you get your homework done immediately after notifications of protest, violence, and civil unrest? Envision scrolling through social media and bearing witness to your friends' severe mental health crises. You want to be there for them, but their texts and posts are interrupted by news flashes, media shares, and incoming posts about another school shooting or incident of a Black person dying during a police altercation. Grae feared for her life. She and her peers tried to discuss their panic and concerns with various adult supports, including their parents, teachers, extended family members, siblings, neighbors, and whoever else would listen. They tried to talk with their trusted adults about depression, anxiety, and terror that felt so real to them even though it was mostly on the other side of a screen. Their new paranoia lived behind face masks in quarantines. They were not permitted to interact face-to-face with people. Grae felt dragged away from society and trapped at home, "watching all this bad stuff happen." Teachers did not address it in the classroom. They did not change when tests were scheduled to take place or when homework was due. It almost made Grae wonder if it was real to begin with.

Upon reflection, Grae expressed that she needed the adults in her life to be honest and vulnerable with how they were feeling (Ask #1, Be as Honest and Vulnerable as Possible), and she needed them to be accepting of her feelings too (Ask #3, Practice No Judgment). She sought validity in her words and thoughts to cope with her feelings of powerlessness (Ask #2, Respect Boundaries and Thresholds). Were Grae's asks of us too much? Do adults know the difference between blocking and controlling exposure to crises as opposed to transparently supporting youth in processing crises? Problem solvers and caregivers struggle with not knowing how fix issues that youth are facing and find discomfort in just being present with youth through their suffering, including and especially children and young adults. There may not be such a thing as the right words in times of chaos (Ask #6, Respect the Process of Learning the "Right" Language) as the real and ongoing work of creating safer, braver, and more courageous spaces generates more questions than answers (Ask #8, Grant Permission to Go Deeper or Decline).

Walking the Chaordic Path with the Nine Asks

There is no cookie-cutter, one-size-fits-all way we can and should seek application of the Nine Asks, especially with young people and in learning spaces. Lottie's and Grae's narratives demonstrate how each individual's story informs and impacts safety needs and one's readiness to engage in human connection. Find freedom in knowing that safer, braver spaces need customization and nimble application as people and situations change. Below is a list of ways the Nine Asks could have better supported Lottie and Grae as well as other students:

—*Ask #1, Be as Honest and Vulnerable as Possible.* Lottie wanted adults to have some decorum with their honesty. She would have appreciated their personal truths but not to the extent of honesty transitioning into judgment. Grae wanted adults to be honest and vulnerable about issues that she believed warranted feelings and emotional responses. It would have helped to have her own feelings validated.

—*Ask #2, Respect Boundaries and Thresholds.* Neither Lottie nor Grae had healthy, established boundaries. They both would have benefitted from relationships with safer adults to gauge needed boundaries and to understand their emotional thresholds.

—*Ask #3, Practice No Judgment.* Both Lottie and Grae needed mature adults to model that it's OK not to be OK. The students sought permission to experience human emotions, especially the five *f*'s. They needed to know they would not be under scrutiny for being sensitive and for having and expressing feelings.

—*Ask #4, Honor Confidentiality.* Lottie needed consistent experiences from adults in knowing that students had a right to own and tell their own stories. Adults demonstrating the practice of honoring confidentiality would have helped Lottie practice trusting others. Grae needed help feeling courageous to share her experiences and abstract thoughts. It would have also helped Grae to understand the unique position of a mandated reporter when she shared more serious commentary about her mental health.

—*Ask #5, Come Back to Me.* Lottie and Grae both have introverted and empathic temperaments. This means they are naturally inclined to have strong energetic and emotional experiences, but they need time and trust to talk about things. Both would have benefitted from adults understanding how they process information and then circling back to them with curiosity about what they're thinking.

—*Ask #6, Respect the Process of Learning the "Right" Language.* Both Lottie and Grae knew that sometimes the right language doesn't exist. Lottie needed the affirmation when she took the risk to speak up. Grae would have been securely grounded if adults had demonstrated the courage to admit that they didn't have the right answers and had boldly stated, "I don't know."

—*Ask #7, Take the Time to Listen First.* Lottie needed someone to simply make time and space for her, listen to her, and be present for her. She was not seeking answers as much as care and consistency. Grae needed adults to listen closely but not problem-solve before she had an understanding of what she needed to feel safer. She needed a sounding board and a partner with whom she could think and reflect.

—*Ask #8, Grant Permission to Go Deeper or Decline.* Lottie would have felt safer and braver if adults had made her feel worthy of their curiosity and interest. She desired the invitation to be engaged by caring adults. Grae needed more instances where adults granted her permission to seek more insight instead of declining her opportunities to go deeper in conversation.

—*Ask #9, Stay in Your Seat.* Lottie and Grae both wanted adults and caregivers to stay in their seats, but they may have appreciated different forms of adult presence. Lottie may have appreciated a calm, grounding presence, while Grae may have found a protective presence safer and more settling.

Safer Learning Space: Reflection and Considerations

It is not always a matter of saying the right thing but patiently, empathetically creating and sharing space, time, and presence for youth to share their stories (Ask #5, Come Back to Me). Youth are encouraged to be honest with adults (Ask #1, Be as Honest and Vulnerable as Possible). There is an opportunity for us to form a relationship where youth share stories about how they feel and adults support through active listening (Ask #7, Take the Time and Listen First) and trust building (Ask #4, Honor Confidentiality). We must also develop behaviors that reinforce in us a practice of being able to be still in others' discomfort if and when we are chosen as a trusted space (Ask #9, Stay in Your Seat).

Consistency is key. The practice of the suite of the Nine Asks is not a one-time practice. Doing the work means trying, failing, and trying again and again to offer the Nine Asks to others, especially young people, when they need them. It also means we must request the Nine Asks for ourselves, especially as advocates who serve and support youth, when we need to be refueled to prevent our own shut down and burn out. We all need safer spaces to support movement toward healthier learning communities both inside and outside the classroom.

Through the practice of all Nine Asks, there *should* be reciprocity—even between youth and adults. Often, adults share feelings of discomfort about being honest and vulnerable (Ask #1) with youth. They sometimes express that truthful reciprocity in conversation with young people feels inappropriate or like an imbalance of power. On the other hand, if adults do not demonstrate healthy methods of being whole and authentic, when and where will youth learn that authenticity is a good thing? Are we as adults still operating in a do-as-I-say-and-not-as-I-do mode, or are we finally ready to practice what we preach? The practice of safer spaces—day by day and moment by moment—must be fair and equitable. Genuine support, whether in moments of peace or crises, is a vulnerable thing. If possible, this exchange is supposed to be about honesty, authenticity, *and* mutuality.

In Grae's words,

You can't be honest one way and then not get it back. It's not fair. Adults were frustrated with [us] children and asking, "Why aren't you doing your work?" or "I see you're not doing great." Remember, it wasn't only the children that were freaked out; it was the adults as well. That's why there's no such thing as the right words to say. No one knew what to do—including the adults. Think about it; the only people that were there for us and knew what we were going through with us also freaked out. But they were handling it in a completely different way. You can't say stuff to magically make the situation better when it looks like the world was dying. However, if you're an adult and you're being genuinely honest with someone that looks up to you, [just] say, "I have no idea what's going on and I'm scared just like you." You're at the same time, in the same place. When you don't say anything, the kids freak out."

When we as adults are not forthright about our own feelings or vulnerabilities and when we pretend everything is OK, it can appear as though we are passing judgment (Ask #3, Practice No Judgment) on young people for having poor coping strategies. We accuse them of being overly sensitive and emotional about things. This can result in what essentially is described as gaslighting, which is a form of emotional or psychological abuse intending to manipulate the target to question themselves and their perception of reality. Gaslighting was obviously (hopefully) not the intention. However, what we want and what we seek is to be a reputable and worthy guide. Adults sometimes fear that being vulnerable will affect their odds of saying the right thing. We worry about knowing exactly what to do and fear wrong decision-making. Adults stress over perceived or, worse, confirmed incompetence. Sometimes co-creating and co-sustaining safer spaces is not about knowing the best move but just being honest, true, and present. There are going to be periods of time when major changes or crises happen and when everyone is uncomfortable. We must stay in our seats. We must stay connected. We must stay engaged and see the process through with the people whom we profess to love and care about.

CHAPTER 15

Practicing the Asks in Living Spaces

Close your eyes and envision yourself in a place that feels like perfect peace. This place provides you with incomparable safety and serenity. When you are in this space, you are hidden away from all threats that aim to bring you discord. There is a stillness and a quiet in this place that cannot be accessed anywhere else. Here, you feel regulated and rested in your body. Your mind is calm and uncluttered. Your spirit feels expansive and like pure illumination. Now open your eyes. When visualizing this place in your mind, did you picture the place where you currently live? Have any of your previous living spaces felt like a sanctuary to you? The word *sanctuary* has religious roots, but its use has expanded to include anywhere people go for peaceful tranquility or introspection—anywhere a person feels especially safe and serene.

Home from a practical perspective is the location of our shelter, domicile, and (permanent) residence. Experientially and idealistically, home is where we retreat and escape from every other place, including work, school, and our worship spaces. It is the place that shelters us when we sink into the hopeful safety of our own consciousness. Whether home is a house, apartment, condo, or dorm room, where you live and dwell is *supposed* to be your sacred space. Home is where we relax, unwind, and be our most authentic selves. If you live alone, your living space is where you are most sovereign; it is where you have absolute power and control. If you live with others, home is likely where you share space with family, a partner, or close friends. In the best of circumstances, your home includes the people who love the real you and those you love most. The greatest level of vulnerability is expected to be possible and probable at home.

Often, the foundations for our personal definitions of safety start with our social constructs of home. Reflect on your favorite childhood and adolescent memories. Did any of the aesthetics leave a lasting impression on favorite things you still desire and appreciate? Are there objects or habits you like and incorporate in your adult home that originated from your childhood stories and experiences? Take a moment and use memories linked to your five senses to identify how you would describe the feeling of being at home. How does safety and security in your living space look? Feel? Taste? Smell? Sound? Not only do these sensory-based memories help specify our predilections, but they also speak to how we establish cultural preferences and expression. Home is where we first practiced cultural competence.

This book began by proclaiming that no space is purely safe. Consider that even when we are in the privacy of our own homes, many still do not feel 100 percent safe. How is it possible that the location where you have the most control, the most personalization, and the most access to people who know you best still cannot provide guaranteed safety? An overgeneralized way of analyzing living spaces might be through the objects in and around the space. Where is the home located? What is inside the home? Do its objects and areas bring peace, delight, and comfort? It makes sense to incorporate aesthetics in the design and composition of our homes. On further reflection, when people share stories regarding *feelings* about their living spaces—whether positively, neutrally, or negatively—the root and the tipping point of the experience always exists in the relationships with the other humans in the home. Yes, our living spaces involve familiar things, places, and people. However, familiarity does not ensure comfort or the absence of danger and threat.

Threats to Safety in Living Spaces

New research studies regarding young people, including and especially BIPOC youth, are prompting us to reexamine our intergenerational and community connections. Many youths share that when they are distressed, they are more effectively able to relax and decompress through engagement with objects, not people. What does that mean? A depressed or angry teenager may prefer to isolate in their rooms and self-soothe than to share their problems with others. Consider that sanctuary for some young people we care about is better experienced through their movies, music, books, video games, and TV shows than in their relationships with the adults in their lives. We are not effectively making young people feel safer; their belongings do. Now think about the ways we punish youth. Discipline is often administered by taking away their objects. So essentially, they do not feel naturally connected with us. And then when they are disobedient, we disconnect them from the things that matter to them. Balance is difficult. Human engagement is complicated. The danger in establishing order and control at home is that we may inevitably make home the least safe place to be for others.

Personal areas are important safety factors in living spaces. Should the dwelling in its entirety not feel safe, a room of one's own becomes the escape. When folks experience conflict at home or have not successfully landed on an agreed negotiation for safety in a shared living space, the next best thing is to retreat and connect to things and external stories that make them feel safe. We escape through others' lives. We find comfort in social media scrolling, getting lost in a book, binge-watching a favorite TV show through a streaming app, or doing anything that will distract us and allow us to shut off our minds. Personal hobbies practiced in private spaces are generally excellent outlets for peaceful self-care as well. We should be aware, though, that some use hobbies to regulate disruption, especially in living spaces. Personal space matters. Having and finding joy in our personal items matter. The ability to go into one's private room and lock the door might be a significant contributing factor that reintroduces a feeling of safety in a person's nervous system.

What happens when you do not feel safe at home, but you have nowhere else to go? In the absence of having a physical space to close off, folks sometimes opt to shut down. Perhaps the most powerful restart that living spaces provide for a dysregulated person are naps. Have you ever had one of those days when your sanity is contingent upon giving yourself a substantial Control-Alt-Delete by way of a nap? Sometimes we need a little rest because we feel physical exhaustion. Other times, naps provide temporary relief from deeply distressing emotions. This was evident in a conversation regarding living spaces with roommates Ivan and Brooks.

Brooks shared, "A lot of times when I have felt unsafe with other people that I live with at home, I don't have anywhere else to go. I don't have the money to get around. I didn't have any other family members to stay with because my family members are not safe people for me. I've had to be forced to get creative about how to force safety. I just have to make this space feel as safe as I can with what I have. OK, let me burn a candle, because I like candles, the smell, the lighting. I'll read or I'll listen to music, or a lot of times, the safest thing I can do is just take a nap because then I don't feel anything."

Ivan excitedly added, "Sleeping is great escapism. Sleeping is the best escapism."

"Napping is the closest you can get to death," Brooks explained. "Napping is the closest I can get to killing myself [without doing it]."

Ivan empathized. "Yeah, you're not conscious. You don't have to be [conscious]. You're not in your body. There's no guilt, there's no depression, there's no anxiety."

With arms stretched behind his head and eyes closed, Brooks offered, "Nobody can hurt you if you're asleep by yourself. Nothing hurts you and you can't hurt yourself; you're not in your own head."

Did you know that "civilian PTSD" is an identifiable disorder? Many people around the world have the unenviable task of surviving dangerous neighborhoods and communities daily to get to safety. The BBC filmed a news story in 2017 titled "US Inner-City Children Suffer 'War Zone' Trauma" and stated that in some of the most dangerous US communities, 46 percent of residents reported suffering with PTSD compared to 11–20 percent of veterans suffering PTSD from the Iraq and Afghanistan wars.[4] Can you ever be safe in your living space when your community is deemed a warzone? Imagine that just outside your front door or bedroom window, you face drugs, alcohol, addiction, gang violence, shootings, and more.

What about felt safety within households experiencing poverty and disenfranchisement? Imagine that the place you call home is infested with rodents or insects. What if those with whom you reside suffer from mental health or mood disorders that impair them from earning stable income, performing household chores, or maintaining basic hygiene? Can your living space be a sanctuary of safety if you've received shutoff letters from utility companies, past-due bills for credit cards, or eviction notices? For some, reflecting on home through their five senses only recalls traumatic memories: smells of rotting trash, the taste of expired meat, the feel of hunger pangs, the sounds of screams and first responder sirens, the sights of fires, broken glass, and needles on playgrounds. Some have been lifelong neighbors to danger and have never known safety.

People can also be a threat to safety in living spaces. Energy is contagious, both positive and negative. It matters whom you allow to visit your abode. Those who are permitted to permanently share living spaces with you matter even more. When you think of home, images of pleasant objects and joy-giving aesthetics likely come to mind. Deeper pondering often reveals that one of folks' favorite aspects of peace, tranquility, and safety in livings spaces is their healthy relationships with others. Take, for example, a harmonious romantic couple, a loving nuclear family, or a set of cohabitating best friends. Our relationships with those with whom we share a home make or break the safety and security of the experience. The greatest outcome for safety in shared living spaces is being unconditionally accepted and protected while living transparently, honestly, and vulnerably. On the other hand, our definitions of threat and danger can be created or intensified when we trust private spaces with our real, genuine, and truthful identities only to receive rejection by the people who know us best. This is a worst-case scenario, and it happens often, even with family.

If home is where we are most vulnerable, a threat to safety in this place could arguably be the most damaging and disruptive type of terror. Home is thought to be our hideaway for happiness. Home is where we expect to have coverage and protection against the weapons formed against us. What a disruption it is to our foundation when danger calls from inside the house. Think of those who cohabitate with threats like substance misuse, untreated mental illness, violence, various forms of abuse, and other hazards to their health. Even in less severe cases, internal conflict could be the result of lower-level clashes in preferences and coping strategies. Over time, repeated behaviors that conflict with what one considers to be positive and peaceful will impair belief in positive intent. If what I need most is what you desire least and if I continue to meet my own needs, you might perceive that I am a threat to you. Every hero is someone else's villain. It's much easier to consider when others have committed an ought against us. What happens when you are perceived as a threat? What do you do when your behavior contributes to home becoming an unhealthy place for others?

There are more narratives than we can count of people whose most ominous traumas, hurts, and pains were committed by family members. Biological relationships do not always translate to safe, secure, and healthy outcomes. Trauma research such as the Adverse Childhood Experiences (ACE) study demonstrates that we can carry permanent physiological manifestations of trauma in our bodies based on incidents of real or even perceived harm experienced by or before our eighteenth birthdays. Seven of the ten questions on the ACE quiz refer to incidents that would have happened at home.[5] Here are the ACE questions:

1. Did you feel that you didn't have enough to eat, had to wear dirty clothes, or had no one to protect or take care of you?
2. Did you lose a parent through divorce, abandonment, death, or other reason?
3. Did you live with anyone who was depressed, mentally ill, or attempted suicide?
4. Did you live with anyone who had a problem with drinking or using drugs, including prescription drugs?
5. Did your parents or adults in your home ever hit, punch, beat, or threaten to harm each other?
6. Did you live with anyone who went to jail or prison?
7. Did a parent or adult in your home ever swear at you, insult you, or put you down?

8. Did a parent or adult in your home ever hit, beat, kick, or physically hurt you in any way?
9. Did you feel that no one in your family loved you or thought you were special?
10. Did you experience unwanted sexual contact (such as fondling or oral/anal/vaginal intercourse/penetration)?

The wounds we acquire from family members and in a shared living space excavate holes in our hearts that we are sometimes never able to fully fill. We harm others in our family and at home when we do not value, appreciate, and affirm one another. The insecurities some spend their adult lives trying to heal often originated from jokes, insults, or bullying within their nuclear family. Think about the people whose first taste of ostracism, disapproval, competition, being misunderstood, and not belonging started at home with their parents and siblings. When family doesn't feel safe, they become strangers who share our biology. We can develop stranger danger, even with kin.

The psychological safety of children is frail. When they grow up in households that are not emotionally stable, the roots of their seeds for security wither. The long-term impacts can leave unaddressed emotional lacerations and trauma shrapnel in their bodies, minds, and spirits. If we do not aggressively work to restore ourselves and make spaces safer, braver, and more courageous, then epigenetic or generational trauma cycles from one family household to the next can destroy the chance for sanctuary over and over, as seen by

— Grandparents with racist beliefs who were excommunicated from their grandchildren
— A father who was abused as a child later struggling with addiction and incarceration
— A mother who tortured her family and was abandoned on her deathbed
— A sister who was neglected then became a people pleaser and a code-switcher
— A brother who was ridiculed for his weight then developed body dysmorphia

- A son whose masculinity was always questioned and later became an abusive husband
- A daughter who was adultified and became a perfectionist and workaholic
- Children of ultraconservative evangelical Christians who abandon religion in adulthood

How we treat family can impact how they manage relationships with family, friends, and themselves in the future.

The Most Important Asks for Living Spaces

Which of the Nine Asks might we need most when we don't feel regulated in the residence? Most, if not all, of the Nine Asks are applicable and necessary in living spaces. That said, there are certain behaviors that are more concerning in the ways that they disrupt our prospects for peace. These issues require more maintenance than others. Some work is exclusively ours to do, but other obstacles must be addressed by our housemates. Here are several considerations regarding some of the Nine Asks and how the absence of their practice can lead to suffering in the supposed sanctuary.

For Shared Living Spaces

- *Ask #1, Be as Honest and Vulnerable as Possible.* Our roomies see us in our most honest and vulnerable forms. They catch our personality flaws, communication faux pas, and an endless list of other undesirables we'd hoped to keep hidden. Should we perceive that they are bothered, annoyed, or irritated by our authentic selves, it could trigger us to code-switch to make the shared living space more tolerable. Reaching back to my conversation with Ivan and Brooks, Ivan revealed that he began code-switching in childhood for his father's approval. He shared, "I basically erased part of myself to fit other people . . . because wanting to belong is one of the most natural human instincts in the world. You feel unsafe if you don't do [it]. I was stuck in a trap where I either had to erase myself so that I would feel comfortable in the environment or I would be myself, but I [would still] feel uncomfortable. It's a bad situation either way."

—*Ask #2, Respect Boundaries and Thresholds.* If you live with someone who makes you uncomfortable, there is a heightened possibility that your boundaries will be breached more easily. Perhaps you and said person have opposing approaches to comfort and safety, which means you consistently trigger each other's perception of threat. You like the temperature cold, and they like it hot. You prefer quiet, and they enjoy hosting loud get-togethers. You have an avoidant conflict management style, but they want to tackle issues head-on. You are private and not the sharing type. They have an open-door, free-store policy with their room and belongings as well as yours. The degree to which you do not feel safe and the frequency in which you do not feel safe can erode your threshold for discomfort. It is all but impossible to feel safe when it feels as if you share a residence with your antagonist.

For Personal Living Spaces

—*Ask #5, Come Back to Me, and Ask #9, Stay in Your Seat.* Knowing when to circle back for human engagement is an important practice if you live by yourself. Perception draws a fine line between being alone and being lonely. When we have enough time to ourselves, it can become easy to isolate. Never forget that humans are designed to be social and that they biologically crave belongingness. While your solo home may be a perfect seclusion space, the more you excommunicate yourself from human interaction, the greater impact the isolation may have on your holistic growth and wellness. There is a time and place to take moments to ourselves. It is also important to stay connected and stay engaged. The practice of healthy human relationships is just that—practice. Keep training and stay ready.

—Ask #8, Permission to Go Deeper or Decline. Some of the elements of maintaining a living space are a bit tedious. Outside of bills and other adulting responsibilities, the things on the to-do list will always include food acquisition and preparation, laundry, cleaning, and the occasional special projects. Chores can pile up. Health can fail. Life can become overwhelming for no rhyme or reason. Emergencies can pop up that are out of the scope of our subject matter expertise. Those who live with others have a helping hand on-site. When you live alone, problem-solving for your living obstacles can feel overwhelming. Are you willing to ask for help? If someone needs your assistance, are you willing to grant access to space to others? Will you leave your bubble of safety when the call for help comes? Solo living can inspire and encourage fierce independence, but solitude, self-sufficiency, and suffering in silence doesn't equate to safety. We can't have it all and do it all by ourselves all the time.

When Asks Are Well Practiced

Perhaps it is an unrealistic expectation to believe that we can transform a mortal living space into the embodiment of tranquility and serenity. However, there's no harm in adding a little proverbial elbow grease to attempt to consecrate our homes however possible. These spaces are, in fact, different from all the other spaces. It should be set apart. It is the space where we sleep. It is where we cleanse our bodies. It is where we should feel safest to feel our feelings. Our peace, contentment, and stillness are worthy of every good effort.

Co-Creating living space with others. There was an axiom that suggested, "Children should be seen and not heard." That was then, and this is now. It is a fact that people—of all ages—are more amenable to participate and engage when they have choice and voice. When cohabitating with a new partner, have you both contributed ideas to make the space mutually reflective of your taste, or does the space look as if one of you moved into the other's home? When a family prepares to move to a new location, do the children have a vote in which location prevails? Further, when move-in day happens, do the children have creative control over how they decorate their space? Whether use of a democratic process involves selecting the film for movie night or a group effort in choosing the meals for the week, everyone wants to believe that their DNA is engrafted in the place where they call home. Voice and choice are evidence of belongingness and value.

Traditions and routines. Is your home the location for family holiday celebrations? Do you get excited about the passing of the spring equinox signaling it's almost time to tend to your lawn and garden? Where do you gather to watch the big game? Did your family have a cultural practice of playing music and cleaning the house on Saturday morning? Have you ever participated in the practice of using a home kitchen or bathroom as a beauty salon or barber shop? These occurrences and many more are the stories and memories that add to the lure of what makes a house or apartment a home. The living space becomes the incubator where lasting memories are born. Our shared sanctuary, at best, becomes the container and the personification of the Nine Asks.

Invitations—even at home. Before looking at the descriptions of the Nine Asks, we discussed why this framework is called an invitation as opposed to guidelines or rules. The spirit of an invitation communicates intent to welcome someone to engage. The desire to be welcomed doesn't go away once we're home. When folks share a living space, the flow and culture of the house may rush and drag in its communication cadence from time to time. We may forget to extend clear requests for a moment to fellowship with each other. Even under the same roof, different members of the same family may perceive favoritism, neglect, avoidance, and other treatment that doesn't feel good. Stories folks tell about love in action, joy, and belongingness share one thing in common— there was an invitation. You are invited to come to my room. You are invited to share a meal with me. You are invited into a family conversation. You are invited to a family game night. Even when we assume we have access to opportunities for connection, it never hurts to be formally invited.

There is no such thing as normal. Common sense isn't common. One person's ordinary life is another's extraordinary life. Most of our experiences are situational and conditional. Such is the nature of personal stories. Each person's perspective on safety is their own. How we experience living spaces informs our social construct of how safe we do—or don't—feel at home. For some, early memories provided an ideal rubric of peace, joy, and satisfaction for environmental wellness. These folks likely model their current design of home including artifacts or replicas of objects as well as rituals they know to provide refuge. For others, the core memories of safety, especially at home, are as troubling now as they were when they were first created. It is possible that deep reflection could reveal that there is no baseline data for safety. In these instances, as the healing journey begins (or continues), there is also an invitation to create safety in said living spaces for the first time. They may not know what will work and what will fall flat in the attempt to design a sanctuary. The most important thing is trying and striving to feel safe in all human spaces, especially at home.

Special Note

It should not be lost on us that the notion of living spaces is a nebulous concept for those who are unhoused or experiencing housing insecurity. There is an intrinsic value in having a physical address that belongs to you. The independence of having one's own apartment filled with one's own belongings is a critical milestone in adulthood. When one can purchase a house and make it a home, they are blessed with a privilege many never get to experience. Keep in mind that for some, the acquisition of a living space of any kind is their singular prayer for safety.

CHAPTER 16

Practicing the Asks in Faith-Based Spaces

There is no welcome quite like a faith-based welcome, including but not limited to a Christian's church hug, a Muslim's inshallah, or a Buddhist's calm smile. When you are a newcomer, however, nervousness and timidity run through your body. The fear lingers as you anticipate the moment when the dreaded question is asked, "Are there any visitors here today?" And if you tell the truth about who you really are and that you do not know a blessed and sancti- fied soul in the building (except for the person with whom you came, if applicable), you might meekly stand up, give a small wave, and smile without making eye contact. Then the church's particular ceremony of welcoming begins. It could be shaking hands with those within a 360-degree perimeter. Some completely ignore folks' preferences for personal space and go in for the hug. Other churches may even erupt into music with a welcome song from the choir. Regardless of the ritual, the design is to ensure guests feel seen and acknowledged — and for better or worse, it works.

Think about the lengths to which organizations and institu- tions go to welcome someone. For a special guest, they might send people to airports, holding signs with the person's name as an initial welcome. Schools program elaborate orientation weekends and welcome days for new students and families. Businesses orient new employees with a welcome packet and onboarding experience. A new leader in a prominent position might even get a welcome reception, including cards, gifts, and food. We are celebrated for being new, and that feels amazing.

The problem with a gregarious welcome is that it means nothing if the spirit of the welcome cannot be sustained. Have you ever been overwhelmed with kindness and helpfulness when you are new and unknown, then, when folks get used to you, it seems as if you become invisible? The enormity of welcomes is unimpressive if its welcoming gestures cannot be operationalized and embodied as a way of regularly treating people. Many would prefer to have consistent treatment than the unpredictability of wavering acceptance that could end in being shunned or mistreated. Most would rather manage realistic expectations than be given a false narrative of a familial organizational culture and be disappointed later. This especially holds true in voluntary associations like churches, where your consistent participation is not required by student enrollment or an employment contract and where people regularly drift away with very little acknowledgment.

Most human beings ultimately and simply desire to be seen, heard, felt, and appreciated. We want to know that we are not invisible. We want to believe our lives matter. We want to feel connected to other sentient beings. In its altruistic design, the church can do all these things. (Note that the primary lens for this chapter will be Christianity, because that is the tradition with which I am most familiar, but the principles of the Nine Asks apply across all religions and spiritual practices, just as they do in secular spaces.) The church can model examples of perfect love and provide lessons on how to give and receive it. Though there will always be much to debate as it relates to doctrine, the church is an attractive idea. The church complication was, is, and has always been its people. It is filled with glorious, fallible, imperfect people.

Threats to Safety in Faith-Based Spaces

Pastors often equate faith-based spaces to hospitals. They say churches are where people come when they're sick and desire to be well. Being in community with others can feel like a spiritual experience. One might ascertain that a faith-based space should be the safest, bravest, and most courageous of all spaces. We pray to talk and meditate to listen. In quiet moments, we hope to feel the presence of the higher power. Those with spiritual routines may find refuge in their practices. That said, there are also many who anonymously share very different experiences in faith-based spaces. For them, some of the most threatening, fearful, and discouraging environments are in the church. Generation after generation, we hear stories of vulnerable people who were harmed through religious practices.

Though taboo to talk about, a truth for us to contend with is how we utilize and, in some cases, weaponize spirituality. The environments and relationships of faith-based spaces do not always feel safe, brave, or courageous—especially not enough to share with spiritual elders and leaders how unsafe faith culture and climates can feel. Sometimes the power of the title and collar can do more harm than healing. And many times, despite numerous instances when things go wrong in the pulpit, in meetings, or in a hallway conversation, people extend loyalty and devotion to their spiritual leaders. That's what they are expected to do.

The expectation to tolerate and forgive perpetrators and to internalize any perception of danger is what can make faith-based spaces particularly unsafe. Any thought of questioning spiritual texts, leadership, or doctrine is effectively taught to followers to be perceived as fallibility and evidence of a fault in their faith walk. To go against the church, to even question the church, is to put your own salvation at risk. Even in spiritual homes, folks can love and never leave an environment or relationship that is at risk of being threatening, controlling, or downright abusive. Remember, humans are designed to be social with a craving for survival linked to a desire to belong. This is why trauma-informed practices in faith-based spaces are of critical importance.

Deliverance or Danger: Addressing Trauma Responsibly

Imagine that it is Sunday morning and the atmosphere is dense in the sanctuary. Well over two hundred or more people are standing on their feet, swaying as the worship team transitions from belting praise and worship music to keying soft instrumentals. As the service winds down in preparation for the close and dismissal, the pastor communicates that he has it on his spirit to do something he has never done before. He requests all the men to come from the main floor up to the pulpit, which is a large, elevated stage. The most loyal male congregants immediately comply, and he implores the remaining men to follow suit. Slowly but surely, space is made for every male worshiper to stand on stage.

The lower-level sanctuary floor now consists of only women and children. The pastor shares that the Lord wants him to speak to and pray about the trauma all the women in the church may have experienced. He then asks the men, who have joined him on the pulpit, to extend their hands out to pray for the women, who are in front and below them. He also directs the men to ask for forgiveness either directly or on behalf of other men who have harmed, hurt, and abused the female congregants throughout their lives. Not uncommon in evangelical worship spaces, the music continues, and the prayer is ongoing for several minutes. The women initially seem frozen, startled, and unsure of how to react and respond to what is happening. However, the longer the moment lingered, the more the women begin emote.

Women transition from being startled to crying to weeping to wailing. Some even fall out and are cared for by other women on the sanctuary floor. As women continue exhorting prayers, weeping, and shouting random, loud emotional outbursts, the men still stand above and over them. Some continue to pray. Others shift weight between feet, seemingly uncomfortable and not sure what else to do. Eventually after an extended period, the pastor dismisses the men from the pulpit, asking them return to their seats. Shortly thereafter, service is dismissed. Some women take a fair amount of time to leave the church building, exhausted from the emotional release. After that Sunday, the impromptu prayer service regarding women and trauma was never mentioned or addressed again.

This pastor may have had good intentions and a desire to restore safety for women through his impromptu mass prayer service. Unfortunately, it resulted in trauma triggering and threat. The effort was intended to demonstrate advocacy but, in the end, was disempowering. Women were targeted but not considered, given no voice or vote on if or when they desired to spiritually address abuse, mistreatment, and sexual trauma. Men were postured in positions of power, looking down on women from the pulpit and given the authority to pray over them. Children witnessed spiritual chaos without context or clarity. There was also the delicate matter of inadvertently weaponizing God through the pastor's power differential to organize an essentially compulsory spiritual event that led to overwhelming and unresolved trauma, possibly even awakening hidden trauma in some of the women.

A trauma-informed, healing-centered approach would have taken seriously the likelihood that some of the men in the room were actual perpetrators of violence, abuse, mistreatment, and other harm toward some of the women in the sanctuary and that the offering of ministry for women who have experienced trauma might be better offered individually and privately, rather than en masse. If the communal worship context was determined to be appropriate, there might at least be consideration of having women lead the prayer for the other women who had experienced trauma and offering the women the opportunity to pray for the men en masse.

Certainly, in the aftermath of such an unexpected action by the pastor, the church staff should consider offering follow-up conversation, a formal address, or behavioral health-care services to any of the women who may have experienced trauma from the event and implementing a process, whether anonymously or directly, for people to safely share if and why the prayer service may have been uncomfortable for them.

We must be careful not to confuse survival responses, such as fight, flight, freeze, fawn, and flock, with spiritual phenomenon during heightened emotional experiences in faith-based spaces. It is possible that reactions displayed by some of the women could have been a result of both movement of the Holy Spirit and anxiety or panic attacks.

The church and other spiritual spaces could benefit from increased understanding and education on how to create a clear but respectable separation between spiritual practices and behavioral health care. The church is heavily populated with people who have experienced various forms of rather significant trauma. There is great benefit in offering resources for both mental health treatment and faith-based guidance. Imagine the advancement and evolution of faith-based spaces to include professional and board-certified counseling as an auxiliary service or ministry offering. This way, members of faith-based spaces can receive holistic support, spiritual leaders will not be at risk of creating emotionally triggering liabilities on the pulpit, and therapists will not be liable for their patients' faith walks and soul-saving salvation journeys.

Creating Safer Faith-Based Spaces

There is a term in faith-based spaces that speaks to the toxic transformational experience when a spiritual space has become unsafe. The term is *church hurt*. Remember, safety is understood as felt safety, meaning that all the right protocols may be in place for definitive safety (e.g., security staff, doors with locks, etc.) but if a person does not feel safe, that is their reality and lived experience. That is their truth. What happens between the welcome ritual and church hurt that causes people to be harmed in worship and faith-based spaces? How could it be that the holiest of places could be someone's living hell? What's going on when the church saints feel like the most egregious sinners? Where did things go wrong when light turns into shadows? Many have stories about changing faith homes and practices. In some instances, some converted to different beliefs, environments, or religions altogether. When spiritual hurt is deep, severe, and ultimately traumatic, some even opt to withdraw from any and all spirit- and faith-based communities. In rare but existing situations, some fully abandon any belief in the institution of religion or the existence of a higher power.

So, what goes wrong as it relates to worship and faith-based spaces with the Nine Asks?

— *Ask #1, Be as Honest and Vulnerable as Possible.* What happens if the honest and most vulnerable part of who you are represents an identity frowned on by the church? What if you identify as being LGBTQ? What if you live with mental illness? People across all ages, races, income levels, geographic locations, and nationalities share stories of how their religions believed that any sexual orientation, gender identity, or gender expression outside of what is "normal" (i.e., straight and cisgender, meaning that your gender identity matches your assigned gender at birth) is wrong and an abomination in the eyes of God. Mental illness and mood disorders are often linked to trauma and neurological chemical imbalances that can be empirically proven; there are countless stories of faithful people with legitimate and verifiable diagnoses. However, mental illness and mood disorders, such as bipolar disorder, schizophrenia, dissociative identity disorder, and border-line personality disorder, have a history of being treated as demonic possessions. Some believe these kinds of diagnoses are conditions from which one can be "delivered" through sufficient prayer, belief, and faith. Discrediting someone's identity or health conditions deters them from safety in practicing Ask #1, Be as Honest and Vulnerable as Possible.

—*Ask #2, Respect Boundaries and Thresholds.* What happens if a practicing Catholic is not comfortable with the sacrament of confession? What happens if a church goer is advised to seek pastoral counseling but does not trust the pastor with their personal information? Church communities may have structures in place like discipleship that mimic mentorship or apprenticeship as folks seek membership and, in some cases, pursue specific positions of importance and engagement inside the clergy or church community. This may call for a deeper dive into said person's life from leadership within the church. But what if said person does not feel safe or lacks rapport with church leaders? What if paying attention to one's discerning spirit leads them to have an understanding that key members in their spiritual community are emotionally triggered? Is there space and permission to set and honor boundaries in faith-based spaces and adapt practices accordingly?

—*Ask #3, Practice No Judgment.* No judgment is a pervasive issue in many faith-based communities. Many modern churches encourage people to "come as you are." But how many times can you show up to church with *that* hairstyle, *that* makeup, *that* jewelry, *that* outfit, *those* bad habits, *that* social company, or *that* language before someone pulls you to the side either to chastise you or to pray over you in hopes of removing the perceived sin that is causing you to carry yourself in a way that displeases God? We have likely all heard the phrase, "Only God can judge me." Yet, we do a spectacular job of dishonoring Ask #3, Practice No Judgment. We play judge and jury to our fellow worshipers and faith-based practitioners in spiritual service.

—*Ask #4, Honor Confidentiality.* The premise of spiritual and transformational conversion can be very exposing and public, especially for such a personal matter. Take, for example, the practice of altar calls in the Christian faith. A church leader stands at the front of the pulpit and asks those who are willing to bravely step up from their state of safety and anonymity to answer the call of God in front of the congregation for all to see. There is not much confidentiality about stepping forward in corporate worship and, in some cases, being challenged to tell their stories publicly in a format called giving testimony. Are there operational practices in faith-based spaces to ensure members have control over their own narratives?

—*Ask #5, Come Back to Me.* Once the welcome wagon pulls off, does it ever circle back? After baptism, what does follow-up look like? When the conversion is complete, does the church community stay connected? When a church member leaves, especially in relation to difference in opinion or because of an offense, does anyone follow up and work toward relationship repair or even just continued human connection with that person? Or can religious doctrine be used to justify separation from those who don't think or believe the same as us? Religious practices like excommunication, shunning, and the like do not honor the value of all people and, contrary to what some may think, do not make those on the inside any safer.

—*Ask #6, Respect the Process of Learning the "Right" Language.* The long history of religious traditions can make some especially averse to new ideas, expressions, and terminology. Are we ready across all faith-based communities to accept non-binary ways of describing gender? Are we ready to discuss microaggressions, epigenetic trauma, and other weighty topics in the church? Is the church ready to evolve its lexicon to better support the human and spiritual needs of the present and future generations?

—*Ask #7, Take the Time to Listen First.* This Ask begins with a willingness to listen, and sometimes within the church, there is opposition to respecting nontraditional voices as leaders and authority figures on the pulpit and over religious text. This may include female pastors, LGBTQ pastors, or pastors of color. Are youth pastors free to preach to everyone—not only to the teen ministry or Sunday school class? Does a stereotype—or even a doctrine—still exist that would allow us to believe that the only folks worthy of being spiritual guides and faith leaders are the privileged (e.g., straight, male, older, etc.) and that everyone else is relegated to the student lens of listening only? Faithful people of privilege have a lot they can learn from those with disenfranchised identities, if they are willing to listen.

—*Ask #8, Grant Permission to Go Deeper or Decline.* Are we curious to learn more and to truly seek to learn from and understand others, without interest in changing their foundational identity? Do we ask to learn more about folks, not in a way that makes their narrative spectacle and fodder for a perfect conversion story but so that they have power over speaking their truth? Consider the importance of this Ask when bridging differences in power: Does your church allow people to speak truth to power, asking hard questions of leaders and even pushing back on doctrine? Likewise, is the congregation ready to be challenged to go deeper in inquiry and to hold space more safely and bravely for its members and even its leaders?

—*Ask #9, Stay in Your Seat.* This may be the most challenging ask of all for faith-based spaces, given the personal nature and cosmic significance of religious belief. What happens when disagreement and disengagement take place in faith-based spaces? Are spiritual environments safe and courageous enough for people to stay put and work through conflicts, crises of faith, and tragic events? Too often, they are not, because people are not prepared to emotionally regulate themselves and sit in the tension of their own and other people's messiness.

Spiritual and mental burnout is a major concern for pastors, 53 percent of whom have given real consideration to leaving pastoral ministry, according to the Exploring the Pandemic Impact on Congregations study by the Hartford Institute for Religion Research.[6] Leading in faith spaces can be lonely and isolating, largely because the organization as a whole is not operating in a way that makes people feel safe enough, authentic, or brave enough to change and grow. Can religious organizations be authentically sustainable if they cannot find real ways to support the human beings that build, lead, use, and need them?

This is why the Nine Asks are so essential for faith-based spaces. Stories of danger, threat, and discomfort are experienced by countless people but are either internalized or shared in whispers, with no supporting way to process and heal from their religious trauma. But there is hope. Some of the most valuable, meaningful, supernatural, and transformative moments happen in the spiritual- and faith-based community. There is nothing more gratifying than to feel in sync with our higher power during a divine experience where our stories and souls are simultaneously tapped. Our minds can be stimulated in ways we cannot fathom when we explore and research religious texts. Done correctly, faith-based spaces call us to feel more seen, heard, valued, appreciated, and loved than any comparable environment.

CHAPTER 17

Practicing the Asks
in Body, Mind, and Spirit

There is one more space that is critical to examine when thinking about how and where we interrogate safety. It is our inner space. Have you ever paused to think about how safe you feel inside of yourself? Is your body a safe space for you, or is it a space where you have experienced discomfort, threat, hurt, or harm? How is your mind? Are your thoughts and ideas kind to you? Does your mind allow you to have moments of peaceful pause and rest? Or is your mind a place where negative and intrusive thoughts grow wildly like untended weeds? What about your spirit? Is all well with your soul?

Best practices and applications of the Nine Asks call for us to be at or above holistic wellness capacity. It is imperative that we understand how it feels when we are at our best, what happens when we're at worst, and what are some of the most effective ways to move back toward optimal health. Self-care is one of the wisest teachers for instruction on the co-creation of safer spaces. Increased knowledge in self-compassion is also an incomparable asset for our collective continuous improvement process in building empathy to be attuned listeners and credible storytellers. Not only can the Nine Asks be a vehicle for human engagement when we're well, but it can serve as an exemplar for "what love looks like in public," as referenced by American philosopher, theologian, political activist, and public intellectual Dr. Cornel West through his definition of justice.

When we do not feel safe, levels of stress and distress can escalate and manifest in our holistic health and wellness. Assume internal application of Ask #1, Be as Honest and Vulnerable as Possible, about our health is a baseline for all ways we experience illness and wellness. Further, observation of our body, mind, and spirit-based warning system is a prerequisite for Ask #2, Respect Boundaries and Thresholds. The Substance Abuse and Mental Health Services Administration (SAMHSA) offers a model of health called the Eight Dimensions of Wellness.[7] This framework approaches wellness from a holistic perspective and gives suggestions on all the ways we either can be unhealthy or can lean into an improved quality of life. Think of these dimensions as engines through which we can also witness the demonstration of the Nine Asks.

— *Financial wellness* explores the health of our relationship to and management of money, a graceful opportunity for Ask #3 to practice no self-judgment.

— *Occupational wellness* gauges how we feel about our job and career satisfaction and is a prime moment to lean into Ask #5 and return to our dreams and aspirations.

— *Intellectual wellness* examines the expansiveness of our cognitive and creative outlets as Ask #6 reminds us to be patient with ourselves about learning processes.

— *Environmental wellness* considers the aesthetics of pleasant places and things around us like discovering our inner sanctuary when we ground ourselves in Ask #9.

— *Emotional wellness* analyzes coping strategies for feelings and management of emotions. Ask #1 and #4 complement this dimension through honest and vulnerable reclamation of our wellness stories.

— *Social wellness* looks at our connection and belongingness to people in our lives, and better linkages require the careful listening to self and others through Ask #7.

— *Physical wellness* encompasses practices such as eating, sleeping, and exercise habits that can be strengthened through boundary setting as we improve in Ask #2.

— *Spiritual wellness* probes the meaning, purpose, balance, and peace in our lives with hopes that something great in us and greater than us is stirred through Ask #8.

Take a moment to assess your overall well-being through these eight categories.

Threats to Safety in Our Bodies, Minds, and Spirits

If we confess to a moment of transparency with ourselves, sometimes we are not OK. It is OK to not be OK. In fact, low moments are ideal times to implement the Nine Asks and request the support you need to feel safer and more stable; it's exactly what they're for. It is healthy to be honest when we do not feel solid, secure, and stable; we just need a little Ask #1. When we can't articulate a feeling of emotional gravity directly but we know how it feels when we are not at our best, we likely need Ask #5 or Ask #7. In moments when we explain away a lack of internal comfort and safety by telling others and ourselves that we are tired, underneath the fatigue is a need for Ask #2 and a hope someone offers Ask #8. The Nine Asks are available to us whenever we need them most.

Which of the following types of tired are you experiencing:

— Brief exhaustion is linked to surface-level stressors, such as work and home responsibilities, and may be a notification to revisit safety in your body. People in your human systems can support this need by offering Ask #1 and Ask #2.

— A season of overwhelm, especially amid the completion of a larger task, such as a major event, a work or school project, or preparation for a difficult duty, may be an alert to return to safety within your mind. Protocols of behavioral health-care professionals are imbued in the virtues and safety protocols of quite a few of the Nine Asks.

—Exhaustion linked to deeper hurt and harm, such as a devastating hardship, tragedy, or trauma in your life (which may or may not have healed) could be a warning to restore safety in your spirit. Lean on those you love and trust most—or start with you—and boldly demand each of the Nine Asks as often and for as long as you need them.

Body Check-In When Physically Tired

Stories of safety, threat, and discomfort are housed in our bodies. Deprivation of these basic human needs often translates into internal allergic reactions within our vagus nerve, which controls major functions like our nervous, respiratory, circular, and digestive systems. Perpetual hypervigilance and dissociation create extensive wear and tear within bodies that are housing stories rife with hurt and harm. Be aware of the SOS distress signals your body pings to you when it is in pain. These vessels of ours are excellent barometers and early detectors to let us know where we lacked the opportunity to be beneficiaries of safer spaces. The Nine Asks, ideally exemplified, can be a universal balm. What and how you feel might assist in telling you which Ask(s) you need. When we are denied access to virtues like honesty, confidentiality, time, a listening ear, and appreciation, we may successively encounter physiological distress, such as:

- Anger
- Anxiety
- Back pain
- Burnout
- Changes in eating
- Chest pain
- Crying spells
- Depression or sadness
- Feelings of insecurity
- Forgetfulness
- Headache
- Heart palpitations
- High blood pressure
- Irritability
- Lack of focus; distraction
- Lowered immunity
- Relationship issues
- Restlessness
- Sleep problems
- Smoking or drinking
- Upset stomach
- Withdrawal from people
- Worrying

Mind Check-In When Mentally Tired

We cannot hand out benevolence in the form of the Nine Asks when our own cups are empty. Decision fatigue, depletion of your battery, intellectual overstimulation, or the conversation bank hitting insufficient funds indicate the need for a brain break. Before you get to the point of readiness for human engagement, you may simply need to rest. Sometimes we plan a much-needed rest session only to feel just as exhausted as we did before the reprieve. Ask #5, Come Back to Me, alone won't satiate mental exhaustion. If we're too tired, we don't know how to respond to Ask #6, Respect the Process of Learning the "Right" Language, or Ask #8, Grant Permission to Go Deeper or Decline. And if we're tired of talking, Ask #7, Take the Time to Listen First, is moot. The problem could be that you need a specific kind of rest for the specific kind of mental exhaustion you are experiencing. Researchers are now suggesting that there are multiple forms of rest—seven, according to Dr. Saundra Dalton-Smith.[8] Review the following categories and determine which one best suits the relief your fatigue needs to recover fully and adequately:

— *Physical rest* involves restorative activities that allow the body to reduce fatigue and give it time to repair, recover, and rejuvenate.

— *Mental rest* allows us to unplug from cerebral stimulation and have time to recharge and process information for better focus, productivity, and alertness.

— *Emotional rest* implements self-care practices for better balance to support de-stressing, avoid or reverse emotional burnout, and allow time to process feelings.

— *Sensory rest* supplies a detox from overstimulation and overexposure to light, noise, and other sensory inputs to reduce sensory overload and overall stress.

— *Creative rest* offers a pause from required or mandatory productivity, problem-solving, and creating to replenish chosen inspiration, innovation, and motivation.

— *Social rest* affords intentional isolation for a break from social engagement to recharge, regulate after burnout, and reestablish the practice of healthy boundaries.

—Spiritual rest grants time to connect to the inner self and reflect on the purpose and meaning of our lives for holistic grounding, centering, and personal fulfillment.

When our minds are busy, we are too distracted to notice the still, small voice and its invitation to rest and recuperate. Mental exhaustion means you are ready to lean into some self-care efforts to get your mind quiet. The Nine Asks are all about permission. Similarly, mental rest allows silence to be a voice and gives us permission to explore and enjoy our personal time. Below is a tool I created in 2017 for mindfulness and reflection implementation called S.A.A.V. (Silence as a Voice) Time through Personal Practices. Hopefully this list will inspire you with activity ideas to get you started in identifying outlets for meaningful rest. Pick a practice and add it to your self-care tool kit. Once you know what brings you serenity and restoration, use the Nine Asks to regularly respond to your holistic wellness needs.

S.A.A.V. (Silence as a Voice) Time through Personal Practices

— Assembling Puzzles
— Coloring
— Cooking
— Craft-Making
— Dancing
— Daydreaming
— Doing Pilates
— Drawing/Painting
— Floating in Saltwater
— Getting a Massage
— Grounding
— Journaling
— Listening to Music
— Meditating
— Napping
— Playing Board Games

— Playing an Instrument
— Playing Video Games
— Practicing Guided Visualization
— Practicing Yoga
— Praying
— Reading
— Receiving Reiki
— Running
— Singing
— Sitting in Salt / Halotherapy
— Sound-Bathing
— Taking a Nature Bath
— Watching a Movie
— Walking

Just as physical safety requires rest, our minds need rest too. There are multiple forms of rest; therefore, do research and practice as many as you can to personalize your awareness on what makes you feel regulated and at ease. Know what works and figure out when you need specific forms of rest to respond to the kinds of unrest your body is experiencing. When your mind feels safer, it is easier to consider—and be positively responsive to—the mental safety of others. Easing threats in our minds takes a little more time and attention to achieve.

Spirit Check-In When Spiritually Tired

When we don't trust or know how to access our own internal safety, it is difficult for anyone else to make us feel safe. We may struggle to be present and responsive to others' needs too. Spiritual healing requires a great deal of our time, attention, pain excavation, and an endless amount of grace, acceptance, and forgiveness, both externally and internally. Though there are tremendous benefits that accompany soul restoration, most avoid deeper dives into shadow work. Spiritual unrest is the deepest disruption and requires an introspective journey to discover—and mend—the root causes of our pain and exhaustion. Often, its journeymen are guided back to the lofty assignment of restoring old relationships and repairing old wounds. This can take the form of parental and family counseling, ancestral lineage healing, or inner-child healing and re-parenting oneself. It's worth it, but it hurts and it's hard. The good news is even when we're afraid, we can do hard things.

Healed Inner Child, Healthy Grown-Up: Teagan's Story

Felice, a type A power executive, and Teagan, a self-proclaimed hippie, served as leads for a community project. There were glaring differences in personality, communication style, and work approach, but the bright professionals had a mutual respect regarding tenacity, compassion, and giftings. Soon after the project launch, Teagan was faced with an unexpected personal crisis and was wrought with overwhelm and anxiety. When physiological manifestations, including headaches and insomnia, became too noisy, Teagan had no choice but to be honest with herself that she needed to seek professional help.

In the absence of being able to identify the right therapist fit and support, Felice offered Teagan coaching services as a bridge until she was able to find another provider. Felice was credentialed to counsel and coach; however, Teagan was apprehensive about mixing a work relationship with a personal coaching service. Desperate for professional support, she acquiesced and accepted Felice's offer. In their coaching sessions over the next several months, Teagan asked for what she needed: improved mental health; Felice shared that she would also be inserting business coaching in the sessions to help Teagan get out of her own way and be a better business professional. The sensitive servant leader felt discomfort with Felice's opinions but doubted her own intuition and moved forward with the coaching.

Felice's coaching was theoretically instructive and heavily resourced, but something was wrong. Teagan didn't feel helped; she felt hurt and engorged with worthlessness. She decided to incorporate her own ancestral memory of healing practices to recreate internal safety within her mind, body, and spirit. In the absence of easily identifiable childhood memories due to dissociation, Teagan used mindfulness meditation and somatic exercises to interrogate her conundrum with Felice. She started with her body. After coaching sessions, Teagan felt tension in her arms, heat in her face, butterflies in her belly, and tightness in her throat. Mindfulness meditation guided Teagan in remembering extreme discomfort and conflict a few years back with an office mate who insulted her expertise and professionalism. She sat still with her recalled memory, graced the pain, and gave herself time to breathe, journal, and reflect on the experience. In another mindfulness meditation sitting, Teagan retreated further in her mental recesses and recalled a clique of young women with whom she sometimes socialized in college. This ingroup occasionally joked at Teagan's expense about her style, sense of humor, and neurodivergent quirks. She remembered body discomfort in the presence of her college peers that mimicked how she felt during coaching sessions with Felice. She acknowledged the sensations, honored the vulnerability of the source, and used additional self-care practices to let go of the pain and hurt.

Days later, Teagan merged meditation and prayer to search herself for any other memories that needed to resurface. Finally, the core memory from elementary school ascended; a tear snuck past Teagan's closed eyes as she remembered a group of kids from her fifth-grade class terrorizing her for being sensitive, soft, and weak. Though she'd begun life as a quiet but confident child, this traumatic incident implanted in her feelings of shame and guilt for having more artistic ability and sensitivity than fighting skills and street credibility. Suddenly it all made sense! Teagan now knew the reason why her coaching wasn't clicking. Felice felt threatening and unsafe to her. The energy and approach of the coaching reminded Teagen of a pattern of social situations where she felt unworthy, unappreciated, and pressured to code-switch for belongingness and acceptance.

Once Teagan was able to mentally envision the story of what happened to her and give her body an explanation for its dysregulation, she knew what her spirit needed to reset, reestablish internal safety, and heal. It wasn't just the grown woman who was hurt and angry; her inner child was still wounded from multiple incidents of rejection for being genuine. Both grown-woman Teagan and little-girl Teagan needed to feel safer and braver in their authenticity.

In the coaching session that immediately followed Teagan's inner work, she shared her observations with Felice, who seemed to acknowledge and note the concern. However, during a virtual team meeting within a week of the epiphany, Teagan was again disrespected and devalued. The incident attempted to disempower her as a leader. Clear now of what she needed to reestablish safety, Teagan started with brave self-advocacy and resigned from the work project, coaching, and all personal contact with Felice. Time moved on. Anger-filled days turned to weeks of honoring feelings of pride, hurt, grief, and relief. Eventually, grown-woman Teagan settled into a place of peace with the resolution. And little-girl Teagan, her inner child, delighted in newfound safety, finally feeling seen, heard, believed, and protected. Teagan was gentle with herself through small demonstrations of grace, acceptance, and forgiveness—internally and externally. She, for this season of healing, allowed silence to be a voice in her self-care activities. She told herself (and reminded her inner child) that there never were—nor are there now—any flaws in her design. Teagan is a different kind of leader than Felice, and that's OK. The world is big enough for both of them.

The internal application of the Nine Asks is guaranteed to be silent, sometimes scary, and almost always spiritual. Identifying internal safety (especially if you've never had it or trusted it) may feel like getting lost in the wilderness. Now substitute *lost* with the word *protected*. You are not lost; the wilderness is your divine covering and practice lab to figure out how to create and design your greatest self-care strategy. Teagan's meditation sessions forced her to establish a routine of trusting herself and her ability to be a safe enough space for the true message of her greatest burdens and blessings to reveal themselves from within the wilderness. By navigating some of her danger, discomfort, and threat stories, she discovered a pattern. She was susceptible to a specific kind of hurt and harm, which meant that her Asks moving forward needed to be customized uniquely for her healing journey. The root cause, source, or origin story of her trauma started in childhood. Therefore, rescuing and healing her inner child was the main prescription and the missing link for her holistic wellness treatment plan.

We are worthy of regularly practicing how to treat ourselves with more gentleness, care, and grace. Reflect on the affirmations below for ideas on how to establish and maintain internal safety:

Nine Asks Affirmations for My Internal Healing

1. *Ask #1, Be as Honest and Vulnerable as Possible,* emancipates me from suffering in shame, guilt, or denial about my own truth. I can be honest and thorough in the interrogation of my deepest pain points, knowing that when I understand the source of my hurts, I will have a better idea of how to heal.

2. *Ask #2, Respect Boundaries and Thresholds,* stretches me to face my fears and yet know when enough is enough. I can and will bury dead relationships and practices that bear no fruit. Learning what it feels like to have capacity and room to expand in my mind, body, and spirit will be one of my most valuable harvests.

3. *Ask #3, Practice No Judgment,* reminds me to extend myself internal grace, acceptance, and forgiveness when I unfairly judge myself. There is nothing wrong with being soft.

Sensitivity is not a flaw. None of my quirks are mistakes or accidents. I am worthy of being provided with a soft place to land instead of harsh judgment.

4. *Ask #4, Honor Confidentiality,* beseeches me to use my voice as the main character, author, and the most powerful narrator of my story. There is a sacredness to my story, and my assignment is unique to me. I don't need the approval of others to take up space. I feel no pressure to control or inform others' narratives of me. I am the only person qualified to be me.

5. *Ask #5, Come Back to Me,* soothes my predilection to rush to actions and decisions when I need to feel the compassion of my own pauses and patience. I will routinely check in with myself regarding my wants, needs, values, thoughts, beliefs, temperament, and energy flow for consistent awareness of and grounding in how my own love feels.

6. *Ask #6, Respect the Process of Learning the "Right" Language,* grounds me when I am at risk of allowing perfectionism and insecurity to make me take up too much or too little space. It took time for me to collect and acquire my hurts and lessons. I will allow an authentic process to unfold of naming feelings, memories, and experiences boldly and accurately.

7. *Ask #7, Take the Time to Listen First,* slows me down before I interrupt my own feelings with coulda, woulda, shoulda and negative self-talk. When I take time and am patient with myself, I realize that my body, mind, and spirit are in constant conversation with me. They deserve time, attention, focus, and compassionate listening to teach me what I need.

8. *Ask #8, Grant Permission to Go Deeper or Decline,* allows me time to ask myself the deeper questions and reestablish safety in self-interrogation. I can also decline going deeper when I don't have the capacity. I can do hard things. I can thrive after survival. I am open to developing a connection with a version of myself I don't know and have never met or been before. And no is an acceptable answer to others and to myself, whether my reservoir is empty or full.

9. *Ask #9, Stay in Your Seat,* regulates and redirects me through mindful self-care when I try to disconnect through

dissociation or hypervigilance. I accept, commit, and submit to healing's iterative process, aware that it will hurt and consecrate. I cannot and will not quit on me. I will see this process through from my inner child to my inner elder.

Feeling unsafe within ourselves is a common but incredibly challenging phenomenon. What do you do when you are the person whom you do not trust? What if the threats to your safety are your own treatment, thoughts, and behaviors? The onset of stress, overwhelm, and burnout can trigger old feelings and emotions in our bodies, minds, and spirits. Sometimes deeper things are awakened in us when we feel unsafe—old feelings of threat. We may recall people we trusted who betrayed us. Feelings of disappointment may creep up from times when we took risks and were let down. Disruption may even cause us to question ourselves, who we are and who we believe we are trying to be and become. For some, painful memories of occurrences when we were endangered stay locked away for an undetermined amount of time. For others, every detail resurfaces through our experiences and stories. Regardless of what we can recall, our bodies "keep the score" as Dr. Bessel van der Kolk says.[9] Our bodies remember moments in our lives, especially during childhood, when our needs for safer, braver, and more courageous spaces went unmet.

In Conclusion

Before you put this book down and get started on the next task from your things-to-do list, BREATHE. Just breathe. Breathe deeply down to your navel. Fill your chest and belly with good news. Sit still and take a moment to affirm yourself and this body that has done its best to carry you through 100 percent of your days as of this moment.

We built the container. We accepted the invitation to practice the Nine Asks. We considered the application of the Nine Asks in various spaces. So what? Now what? If you're struggling with where to start on your Nine Asks trek, reflect on these ten quick check-in/check-out questions:

1. How would you describe ideal safety today?
2. When was the last time you felt brave?
3. What's your current do-it-afraid challenge?
4. What are you learning about childhood you versus the adult you?
5. How are your five *f*'s showing up when you're not OK?
6. Who was on your heart or mind when reading this book — and why?
7. What feels alive and awake in you right now?
8. Where are you still blocked, hesitant, or resistant?
9. What kind of tired are you, and how long have you been tired?
10. Which of the Nine Asks do you need right now?

As you ponder on where to start, I want to end by saying, thank you. I am grateful for your willingness to submit to the process and exploration of the Nine Asks. Be kind and gentle with yourself on this new journey. Show yourself profound compassion when you fall and honor every time you get back up and try again. I extend gratitude for who you are, what you are being called to do, and which gifts you have been given to channel your assignment. I see you. I affirm you. You got this!

And it is so.

Amen and *Aṣ́é*.

NOTES

1. Frank Edwards, Hedwig Lee, and Michael Esposito, "Risk of Being Killed by Police Use of Force in the United States by Age, Race-Ethnicity, and Sex," Proceedings of the National Academy of Sciences, August 5, 2019, https://www .pnas.org/doi/10.1073/pnas.1821204116. The report states that the risk is high-est for Black men, who face about a one in one thousand chance of being killed by police over the course of their lifespan.

2. Chimamanda Ngozi Adichie, "The Danger of a Single Story," TED, October 7, 2009, https://www.youtube.com/watch?v=D9Ihs241zeg.

3. Microsoft Canada, "Attention Spans," Spring 2015, https://dl.motamem.org /microsoft-attention-spans-research-report.pdf.

4. Franz Strasser, "US Inner-City Children Suffer 'War Zone' Trauma," produced by Ashley Semler, BBC News, December 6, 2017, video, 3:42, https://www.bbc.com /news/av/world-us-canada-42229205.

5. Office of the California Surgeon General, "Adverse Childhood Experience Questionnaire for Adults," May 5, 2020,https://www.acesaware.org/wp-content /uploads/2022/07/ACE-Questionnaire-for-Adults-Identified-English-rev.7.26.22.pdf.

6. "'I'm Exhausted All the Time': Exploring the Factors Contributing to Grow-ing Clergy Discontentment," Exploring the Pandemic Impact on Congregations, https://www.covidreligionresearch.org/wp-content/uploads/2024/03/Clergy_Discon tentment_Patterns_Report-compressed_2.pdf.

7. Substance Abuse and Mental Health Services Administration, "Creating a Healthier Life: A Step-by-Step Guide to Wellness," 2016, https://store.samhsa.gov /sites/default/files/sma16-4958.pdf.

8. Saundra Dalton-Smith, *Sacred Rest: Recover Your Life, Renew Your Energy, Restore Your Sanity* (New York: FaithWords, 2017).

9. Bessel van der Kolk, *The Body Keeps the Score: Brain, Mind, and Body in the Healing of Trauma* (New York: Viking, 2014).

www.ingramcontent.com/pod-product-compliance
Lightning Source LLC
Chambersburg PA
CBHW021456050325
22877CB00002B/2